PREJUDICE AND PRIDE

LGBT ACTIVIST STORIES FROM MANCHESTER AND BEYOND

LGBT YOUTH NORTH WEST
EDITED BY CLÍODHNA DEVLIN

HAMMERON PRESS

COPYRIGHT

PREJUDICE AND PRIDE: LGBT ACTIVIST STORIES FROM MANCHESTER AND BEYOND

First published in 2015 by HammerOn Press
http://www.hammeronpress.net

British Library Cataloguing in Publication Data
A catalogue record for this book is available from the British Library

Prejudice and Pride: LGBT Activist Stories from Manchester and Beyond
selected by LGBT Youth North West and edited by Clíodhna Devlin
1. Lesbian, Gay, Bisexual and Trans* History 2. Public History. 3. Social and Community History.

ISBN-13: 978-0-9564507-8-4
ISBN-10: 9780956450784

Cover design and layout
by Tamzin Forster
www.tamzinforster.co.uk
Typeset by Tamzin Forster in
Misproject by Misprinted Type
Eduardo Recife
Crash Waves Lead To Skinny by Skydog
Handwriting Dakota by
Altsys Metamorphosis
League Gothic by The League of Moveable Type

HOW YOU MIGHT WANT TO USE THIS BOOK...

You can read this book on your own or in a group, dip in and out, read from cover to cover, go off and do more research in the topics that interest you, pass it on to friends and family, or buy more copies for folk who you think might want or need it.

If you are new to the idea of activism, or taking action against things you don't agree with, then we hope this book will inspire you. If you already are an activist then we hope it will give you the courage and strength to continue your important work.

There are activities in the book you can engage with if you want to, or share with others. If you are an educator (youth worker, teacher, parent etc), then please pass on the ideas and information in this book.

If you come across a quote in the book and you want to know more about who said it, there are short biographies about each person at the back of the book.

Here are some common words that will come up in the book:

Lesbian: A woman who is physically and/ emotionally attracted to other women.

Gay: A man who is physically and/ emotionally attracted to other men (although sometimes women who have same sex attraction also refer to themselves as gay).

Bisexual: Someone who can be physically and/ emotionally attracted to either men or women.

Heterosexual: Someone who is physically and/ emotionally attracted to someone of another gender e.g. A woman attracted to a man, or a man attracted to a woman. (This is also known as 'straight'.)

Trans*: Someone whose gender is not the same as it was presumed to be at their birth, or their gender does not fit with Western society's ideas of 'man' or 'woman'. This includes people who are transgender, transsexual, transvestites, or non-gendered people.

Cis-gendered: someone whose gender matches the one it was presumed to be at their birth e.g. someone who feels like a woman inside and was presumed to be female from birth.

IN MEMORY OF...

In memory of two activists who dedicated their lives to campaigning, educating and empowering themselves and others to support the LGBT Community, in Manchester and beyond.

GEMMA GODDEN REMEMBERS HER WIFE, JAYE BLOOMFIELD (1969-2013)

Jaye Bloomfield

Jaye was born in Ipswich and her activism started young - in the '80s she was kettled by the police at Anti-Nazi demonstrations in London.

Jaye always stood up for what she believed in. Her first visit to Manchester was as an LGBT union representative for the PCS union. She was proud of her union involvement. She moved to Manchester in 2002 for the LGBT scene (as well as the music).

I met Jaye in 2004 at the re-launch of Manchester City Council's LG employee group. We got involved in the Core Group and successfully campaigned for the group to become an LGBT employee group. We also pushed for all the equalities documents across the different departments of the council to recognise and meet the needs of LGBT people.

Jaye brought her design skills and sense of humour to the role - she designed the posters, updated the intranet site and worked hard to push things forward. I researched and had facts and figures to back up proposals - Jaye had the passion and confidence to put points across verbally. We made a good team.

Jaye was outspoken - she said what was on her mind and was honest to the point of bluntness. She used humour often and brought a lot of laughter. I remember once when a man shouted "lesbians!" as we walked down the street holding hands – Jaye pointed at him and shouted "heterosexual!" She then had to explain what heterosexual was to him. He shuffled off looking a bit embarrassed.

From 2004 to 2008 we organised launch events for LGBT History Month, arranged for trans* and bisexual speakers to attend our meetings and attempted to make the meetings more accessible to LGBT women, people with disabilities and Black and Minority Ethnicity (BME) people.

Jaye always believed in standing up for your rights – at our wedding she thanked all the activists whose work had allowed us to get civilly partnered as she knew that without them we wouldn't have had that beautiful and important day.

A song that she loved and which sums up Jaye's attitude is 'Raise' by Bocca Juniors:

"Raise your voice, you'll be spoiled for choice, just stay quiet and you won't."

The day before Jaye died she told a friend to get her union involved as she was having problems at work "If you don't do something, nuffing will change." The friend did get the union involved and it resulted in improvements for her.

I would love Jaye's legacy to be that she encouraged people to stand up for their rights and to work together to make things better.

IN MEMORY OF...

CAROLE WODDIS FONDLY REMEMBERS PAUL PATRICK (1950-2008)

Paul Patrick

Paul Patrick was passionate, voluble, big-hearted, an inspired and inspiring teacher and one of the country's leading activists on LGBT issues. Above all, he was a human rights campaigner, prepared to challenge all forms of oppression wherever he found them, especially in schools where his impatience with the status quo was vented particularly towards bullying and homophobia.

As a staunch and lifelong trade unionist his influence on his own union, the NUT, helped bring about a sea of change in their attitudes and put them at the forefront of equality for LGBT teachers.

Paul came out in 1969, a courageous act bearing in mind it was only two years after the partial decriminalisation of homosexuality in 1967. In 1974, shortly after starting his teaching career, he helped found the London Gay Teachers Group. Over the years this turned into the campaigning organisation Schools OUT, of which he was the co-chair. He also co-founded LGBT History Month in 2004 with long time friend and work colleague Sue Sanders, and travelled extensively to promote events.

In 1972, he became a teacher at the Roger Manwood School in Lewisham, quickly becoming Head of Drama. One of the first openly gay teachers in the UK, his work soon brought him to the attention of the ILEA (Inner London Education Authority), who co-opted him to serve as an equal opportunities advisor.

His work at the Roger Manwood School set the pattern for what was to become his trademarks: after-school drama projects, pastoral care, training and advice. Under his direction, Roger Manwood School plays became legendary. When the school was amalgamated and became Crofton School, Paul involved at every level in its reconstitution, became its Equal Opportunities Officer, responsible, as later with the ILEA, for advice covering issues ranging from the personal, social and sexual to artistic. It's true to say that Paul spread `good practice' through London schools before the term acquired the fashionable cache it now carries.

In 1997, he moved back North and continued teaching and directing school plays. In the last 2 years he directed, adapted and staged *Much Ado about Nothing* with the Rossendale Players and the British amateur premiere of Eve Ensler's *Vagina Monologues* to great acclaim.

A prolific writer and compelling speaker, he was responsible for many influential training videos: amongst them *A Different Story – the lives and experiences of a group of young lesbians and gay men* (ILEA 1986), the first video to go into schools highlighting homophobic and sexist issues.

In the 1980s he became a foster parent to one of his pupils, an event rare enough to find himself recounting the experience on John Peel's *Home Truths.* It was typical of a person tireless in the cause of human and social equality.

If the roll call of positions he held in the voluntary sector are testament to his irrepressible energy, the heartfelt tributes paid since his death bear witness to the love, respect and admiration in which he was held by people across the spectrum - from teaching colleagues and LGBT community workers to parents, students, artists and, of course, his family.

CONTENTS

CHAPTER 1

WIBBLY WOBBLY TIMEY WIMEY LGBT HISTORIES

NIAMH MOORE

This is a book about the lives of LGBT activists, who may or may not call themselves activists, in the North West of the UK.

It is one of the outputs of a Heritage Lottery Fund (HLF) project in the UK. The project was initiated by LGBT Youth North West, based in Manchester, and partnered with a number of organisations including Schools OUT UK.

This book traces three threads of LGBT activism, loosely based around Manchester and the North West of England, though with attention to how Manchester and the North West are inevitably enmeshed in national and global politics.

The three strands of the project include:

1. the establishment of a purpose-built Gay Centre in Manchester in 1988. This Centre is now managed by LGBT Youth North West;
2. work in schools, supporting teachers and pupils, including the setting
3. up and campaigning of Schools OUT UK (formerly called the Gay Teachers Group);
4. histories of LGBT youth work in Greater Manchester.

Importantly this project focuses on histories of LGBT activism that rarely receive attention elsewhere – the campaigning of teachers, and youth workers. These are particularly important sites for thinking about LGBT activism because they are sites of intergenerational exchange, and thus useful for thinking about change, how change is understood and that what counts as change itself changes over time.

While for some an LGBT history based in Manchester and the North West might seem too parochial, too specific, or merely a small story in a much bigger story, LGBT activists in Manchester have always been ambitious, with a long history of displacing London-centrism, or nationalist narratives, and with a commitment to developing practices, such as in LGBT youth work, which do not necessarily flourish to the same extent elsewhere – LGBT Youth North West after all does

1967	1970	1974
Legalisation of sex between consenting male adults over 21	Homophile Society set up at Manchester University by the Campaign for Homosexual Equality (CHE)	Manchester Gay Alliance starts at the Friend's Meeting House

not have any other regional counterparts in England or Wales. Stories here which are shared LGBT stories, such as those around Section 28, have wide significance because the anti-Section 28 march in Manchester was much bigger than the one in London. The Joyce Layland Centre has, for instance, hosted some incredibly significant visitors, such as Ugandan gay rights activist, David Kato, who was later murdered in Uganda in 2011. In these ways Manchester Gay Centre is deeply enmeshed in acts of solidarity with activists elsewhere.

David Kato (1964-2011)

ORAL HISTORY

This project was funded by the Heritage Lottery Fund in the UK, who have a strong history of supporting community history projects, including LGBT history projects. This was a participatory oral history project, where young people in youth groups were trained in oral histories then interviewed older LGBT activists, teachers, youth workers, and people who had used LGBT services. Oral history projects can allow special kinds of conversations to take place between people, conversations that do not always happen in everyday life. When we tried to suggest to one young person afterwards that she now had skills to go off and do interviews of her own, she astutely recognised that it was not only a matter of skills, but that the project itself created a space to bring people together in ways not always easy to bring about. So this was a special project for all involved which created the possibility for new and challenging conversations all round.

Manchester Gay Switchboard (MGS) begins, first at 7 Birch Hall Lane, then at the Friend office. Gordon Fryer and Terry Waller got beaten up while fly posting for it

Schools OUT UK is founded

1974?

CHE sets up the 'Friend' office at 178 Waterloo Place, Manchester

1975

WIBBLY WOBBLY TIMEY WIMEY

'People assume that time is a strict progression of cause to effect, but actually from a non-linear, non-subjective viewpoint, it's more like a bag of wibbly-wobbly, timey-wimey stuff.'
Doctor Who, 'Blink', Written by Steven Moffat

In our very first session about what LGBT history might be it was already clear that it was a wibbly wobbly picture.

Young people's thoughts on "LGBT History" during first training session, including the first use of the phrase "wibbly wobbly"

The use of the term 'wibbly-wobbly timey-wimey' by one of the young people in our first oral history training session was hardly a coincidence, in a building (The Joyce Layland LGBT Centre) that has often been referred to as a 'Tardis'; such is its capacity to both transport people to different realms, parallel universes, different pasts and presents, and repair rips in the fabric of the universe, as well as its apparently amazing capacity to expand and house a multitude of people and stories over time, and to hold on to the messiness of lives and time.

A curious timey-wimey effect of this project is that though we now know so much more about LGBT histories, we also know more about what we do not

Manchester's Gay Youth Group and Icebreakers (gay men's coming out group) established at Waterloo Place

1975?

£5,000 Urban Aid grant received from Manchester City Council (MCC) and Waterloo Place becomes the Gay Centre.

1978

Transvestite/ Transexual (TV/TS) helpline starts

know, about how we might have done the project differently, about what stories are not included, about how certain stories get told and retold and more marginal stories often require a lot of work and space. These are some salutary learnings. One abiding memory of the process of the project comes from the first 'Memory Day' held in the Joyce Layland LGBT Centre, and as interviews were happening in smaller rooms off the main room, an impromptu focus group emerged as four white, middle-aged professional gay men who had been centrally involved in the early years of the Centre, gathered around youth worker Amelia Lee, filling her in on stories about the history of the Centre, and their involvement. It was a moment of recognition of the capacity of projects such as this to draw people (back) in, of the very different histories of involvement in the Centre, and of power of particular stories, and how some stories get told and others remain marginal, and how it can require significant work to bring these other stories to the centre of attention.

A book such as this also raises intriguing questions about people who do not appear to require some of the support and services that continue to be on offer. This book, and this project, by definition, involves people who have been accessing services and/or been involved in activism. We know less about those who do not appear to have these needs:

'Some people can cope with it, and others can't ... we try to be there for the ones who can't quite cope with it'.

Another noted:

'[we] don't necessarily get people who can find their own way, there have always been people who've said, "Well to be honest with you it's never been a problem, I found my own way, I was perfectly confident, I was out in the village."' [The gay village in Manchester is the pub and club scene based around the Canal Street area.]

Friday night Poly Disco gives an alternative to mainstream gay music scene, continuing into the 1980s

Friend starts a Gay Youth Group, affiliated to the Greater Manchester Youth Association (quite a big deal at the time)

First Manchester Gay Centre Annual Report

1978/9

LIVING WITH HOMOPHOBIA

Like many books on LGBT history, this one too emerges out of complex urges to document ephemeral histories, to try and insist on and mark a series of changes, while at the same time also recognising that there is much work yet to be done, that for most there is still a sense of a need for an LGBT Centre, for organisations like Schools OUT UK. As one participant reflected:

'I just find the whole like politicisation of sexuality weird. I don't know, like it's just weird, why do people care? Why? It doesn't affect them in any way, do you know what I mean? It's just weird.'

Another said:

'When the village doesn't exist, then we will have won. When there's no need for a safe space, why should there be a need for a safe space?'

Meantime there are the effects of decades of living with homophobia and despite a sense of improvements and change, no sense that the job is yet done.

In the project we heard many apparently small stories of living with homophobia, such as how it was experienced through families: 'My dad used to do things like taking me into the garden and making me kick footballs about because he thought that would make more of a man of me.'

The absence of role models, or only limited role models, was a recurring theme:

'Well, I was a teenager in the '60s and so when I was 15 men were sent to prison for four years for being gay. So that meant that there weren't any role models, there was not one single out gay man or woman in the public eye that I could look to and go, "Hey, I can have a happy life." There was nothing, you know, you're taught to hate queers long before you know you are one.'

Manchester City Council funds Lesbian Link helpline, and Gay Centre made more inclusive

Friend and Switchboard receives almost 12,000 calls

Geoff Brighton refused medical clearance for teacher training course at University due to sexuality

1979

'The television images were always negative, there weren't any positive ones. We had no, we had no Jack Harkness or anything like that, I mean we had Larry Grayson and John Inman which didn't really help. 'Cause they were older for a start, so they weren't us, so there was no publicity that we could relate to, there were no icons, there were no role models. All of the role models for young people were straight. ... In those days you didn't have the boy bands or anything like that where they'd, you know, I think it's almost the law that one member of each boy band has to be a gay person.'

Many people we interviewed recounted horrendous experiences, compounded by secrecy:

'I can't even remember the year but it was, I was definitely under 21 so I must have been late teens so it must have been early '60s and I was seduced by this gorgeous man who was posing as my friend and he, I treated him like a friend and he raped me. Erm, and after, I mean obviously it wasn't nice, it hurt, but the hurt was, eventually the hurt was all up in the head. What do I do about this? What do I do? Who do I tell? And I told nobody until, erm, and it must have been mid '80s and I went to a conference... it was a legal conference about, and amongst other things it was about dealing with gay and LGBT clients, how do solicitors deal with, anyway, I went to this conference and I found myself talking at the end of a mic and telling this entire conference of 200 or 300 people in Brighton it was, no it wasn't, it was in Bournemouth, telling people that I was raped as an 18 year old. And I'd never, I'd never told anybody and I even, I shocked myself to hear myself telling this story and it was at a time when male rape was not an offence because male rape didn't become an offence until, and again I might be wrong, but I don't think it became an offence until the late '90s.'

There were significant consequences to living with homophobia:

'Because if you're constantly told that you're abnormal, you start believing it so there was, so there was that, and it was constant. I know I've come back to this

1981		1982
Gay Centre moves to bigger location, 61a Bloom Street, in the now Gay Village	Mancunion Gay magazine launched from Centre	Inner London Education Authority (ILEA Chief Inspector) formally lifts eight year probation on John Warburton recognising teachers' right to be out

a couple of times, but it's very difficult to explain because there's so much less of it now, and the laws have changed so much, but it was a constant battle, every day was a battle of, you know, "oh my God is anyone going to find out today, am I going to lose my job today." Or, you know, "is someone going to beat me up, or is someone going to ban me from a shop or a restaurant," they did things like that, you know.'

Another reflected that:

'The most suicide rates is highest in gay males aged 14 to 18 or something. But I find that most gay children do harm to themselves over other people doing harm, obvious physically not mentally 'cause obviously to be doing stuff physically you will have been damaged mentally by someone else, but like I don't, I don't understand why there isn't that support system there, like there must be some support but it's obviously not prevalent enough for them to turn to it.'

'We'd get stories every day... "the manager doesn't like me 'cause I'm gay, the manager doesn't like lesbians," and, you know, or this, problems at school, someone's found out, or problems at home, they'd get thrown out [of their homes.] That happened to a friend of mine called Albert Kennedy. You may have heard of the Albert Kennedy Trust, well I'm one of the last people to see him alive, playing table tennis on the Saturday, and it was that night he was found in the canal...one friend committed suicide, and that was domestic violence because domestic violence amongst the gay community was

Albert Kennedy, photo from The Albert Kennedy Trust, founded 1989

Lesbian Express launched and runs for 3 or 4 issues

1982? James Anderton, Manchester Police Chief, famously refers to gay people as living "in a cesspit of their own making"

1984 The first 'pride' event – a jumble sale in the village

simply not recognised. It was barely recognised amongst the straight, you know, for women in those days. And we're only talking about 1984 here, it's not the 19th century. Well he was, erm, beaten up by his boyfriend and hanged himself when he was 21, so all sorts was going on.'

A number of activists were explicit about the toll that living and working in a homophobic culture took on them:

'It was that, you know, it was horrible, it was messy. In some senses I was amazed I lasted as long as I did, but I couldn't wait to get out eventually. I think I can say this. I think I'd done some terrific work, and I, I'd got equalities work and LGBT issues kind of really on the agenda, but it was at an enormous cost. I ended up having psoriasis all over my hands and arms, for example, just with stress. And you know, it was just that it kind of burns you out doing that.'

The ability to stay sane was recognised as an achievement, not something that could be taken for granted:

'Staying sane. I've been saying to friends that we met here that it took me about two years after I retired to work out how burnt out I'd become. I mean, I'm so glad that I retired which was partly a matter of being able to afford it and partly a matter of "I think I've had enough," you know.'

Amelia offered a thoughtful reflection on the challenges of activism, not only burnout but also the day to day trauma of gay life for many:

'A lot of the time activists, for example, become activists through a bad experience that they've had and they get angry and they take that out on the world, and that can be a great force for good, but sometimes what it also means is what they haven't done is acknowledge the pain and hurt that they've had. So what they're acting out is still eating them up inside, so I think if people took more time to see how bigotry has affected them and heal themselves, I know that sounds a bit twee, but to heal themselves a bit. I think then in the outside world their interactions are more positive, they can make more change,

Manchester Council's first Equal Opportunities Committee develop Equality and Fairness Strategy.

Manchester Parents Group, now a branch of national group Family and Friends of Lesbians and Gays, formed by 4 mothers of gay teenagers.

UK's first openly gay mayoral candidate Margaret Roff is nominated

1985

your aura is better, people want to be involved in the good stuff you do because they sense that you're more at peace with yourself. So I would wish that I guess for all LGBT people 'cause I think that would help the community.'

CHANGE?

A whole host of changes were identified by participants. These included specific stories, such as around the role of police: 'I think one of the biggest differences in those days, the police used to police Pride, now they're in it, now they have a section in it, they're marching with us.' Others provided extensive reflections of the broad nature of change over time.

Many interviewees went to considerable efforts to try and convey to the young people doing the interviews just how different life had been for them, compared with now. One significant difference many mentioned was the challenge of conveying change in another time with a different culture, when being gay was still illegal. One reflected:

'It's almost like me talking about, erm, the difference between my growing up and someone growing up in Victorian England. I mean the difference between now and the '70s it's... planets away, isn't it? I mean you wouldn't recognise the world in the '70s.'

Another commented:

'I never imagined when I was your age that there would be such a thing as gay marriage. It was just totally, it was totally beyond the realms of reality. It was totally beyond the realms of fiction and even now I think it's, it's just amazing how, what progress has been made. I never dreamt it would actually happen. I mean when people started to talk about it here I thought well that's just pie in the sky, that will never happen and then overnight so much progress was made very, very quickly and we had civil partnerships.'

Manchester 'Pride' held in Sackville Park, with a tombola

Launch of Gay Teachers' Group AIDS leaflets for teachers

Manchester AIDS Line founded at Portland Place – several of those involved with the Gay Centre help set it up

Nigel Leech taken on as a sessional youth worker at Manchester Gay Centre

Peter Cookson also reflected on the almost unimaginable scale of change:

'So I've seen, I've seen things grow and develop, and what I'm most proud of I think is if you'd have said to me in 1984 that there would be openly gay members of parliament represented in the Conservative party, and that it would be virtually illegal to be homophobic, I would have thought you were taking drugs or something. 'Cause a number of my friends got sacked from their job. I was called into my manager's office in 1986, "I've had some complaints... you're too open about your lifestyle." This is the sort of thing that happened. The clubs used to get raided regularly in those days, it's a completely different world, it's a bit difficult to explain to people that have never lived through that, just what it was like. You were in constant fear of, erm, attack or discrimination, even if it was not physical, it was certainly verbal. We, erm, had to be very careful, and the great thing about the youth club was that there were young people that weren't out anywhere else.'

WIBBLY WOBBLY CHANGE

The turn to wibbly-wobbly timey-wimey was wonderfully expressive of a central dilemma of this kind of project. Many interviewees stressed the need to recognise that things are not the same, but at the same time our languages for talking about change can sometimes be quite simple, and we are forced to reflect on whether things are better or worse. The complexities of expressing that life for LGBT might be better and worse and different all at the same seemed to require new words and languages like wibbly-wobbly timey-wimey:

'I think it is easier to be a young person, an LGBT [young person] now than it was 40 years ago when I was, 30 years ago in my 20's, 40... 30 years ago. I can't even get my maths right. But I still don't think, I think it's still for some people, I think, just as difficult so that's the thing we mustn't underestimate.'

First National Conference jointly organised by Gay Teachers' Group and Lesbians in Education

1986

Section 28 of the Local Government Act 1988 enacted and anti-Section 28 campaign launched

1988

Manchester City Council funds a purpose-built Lesbian and Gay Centre at Sidney Street

Amelia Lee reflected perceptively on differences in how people might see change:

'I think for some people but not for everybody there's a bit of a generational thing, so people over the age of 70, 65, 70 will have had some awareness of the time when it was illegal for gay male sex, right? 'Cause that was 1967, 1969 kind of time. So some people still carry that idea of shame and illegality and everything around their attitudes to LGBT people, and obviously those people that are LGBT that are older people also have internalised that.'

Others, like Sally Carr and Jayne Mugglestone respectively, noted that life could still be very difficult, especially for young LGBT people:

'Other things that I guess surprise me are the rise in homophobia in people feeling that they can say things that are homophobic and transphobic. But the level of homophobia that young people face every day, and they tell me their stories when I come here and meet with them, has always surprised me because although there is a notion that things have got better, they have in legislation, but in those lived day experiences the story hasn't changed a great deal.'

'The things that surprise me are that things have not changed very much and I think that's something about working for a long time, so when I was 20, so that'll be 30 years ago. ... I think I mean it as a sad thing really, but if I think about the young women that I worked with then, particular around issues like poverty and discrimination and all that kind of stuff, I just think, "God, it's still going on." So I work with a lot of young women in care, so I look at them now and think this is terrible, we're still not supporting them. Not as youth workers, I think youth workers do, but I think just not having funding from the government, it not being given a priority, people not wanting to put money into it. But then I've had beautiful, beautiful stories, really beautiful stories where you just think, "God, I've hardly given anything to this young person but it's just made all the difference and they've just really blossomed and that's been

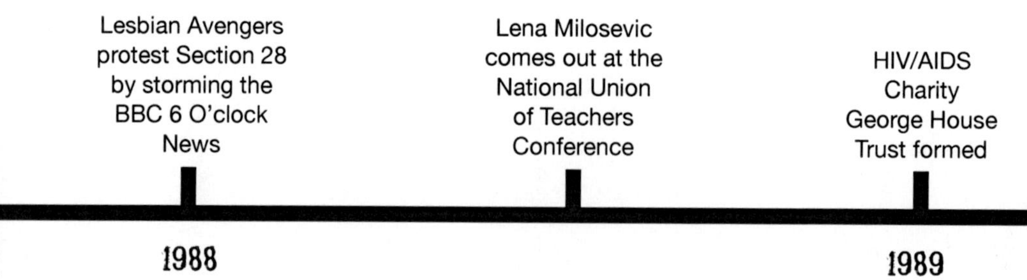

lovely to see." I think actually if we could just change things a little bit it makes a huge difference.'

Sue Sanders, as a long-time Schools OUT UK activist, has a keen grasp of the subtleties of political and social change:

'As LGBT young people have become more visible so too has the bullying, and I believe it's more open and in some ways more prevalent than it has been before because back in the days when being gay for example was illegal, people weren't out, they weren't out at school and they never would have admitted, 'cause it would have been admitted, right? Now when you've got lesbian, gay, bisexual and of course trans* young people coming out at school then there is a whole breed of, what do you call it? Like a backlash against that, of people who can't deal with that. So I think that's a really, a new issue we've got to really challenge I suppose. ... Yeah, I think it's a mixed picture. It would be a lie to say that things have just got better. Progress doesn't just happen because time happens and it doesn't just happen 'cause laws change. So if we don't continuously do work within our own communities and our culture then we can't expect stuff to change. And stuff like the rise of the use of the word gay, and that being considered acceptable in a lot of places, shows how sometimes bigotry just takes on a different face.'

Janet Batsleer also puzzled over the paradox of, on the one hand substantive change for LGBT people, and on the other hand ongoing challenges in living as an LGBT person, especially as an LGBT young person. She points to the huge importance of families in shaping, determining, and sometimes constraining young people's lives:

'And you know, we've got gay marriage and in some ways things have changed out of all recognition. There are still young people growing up who face a sense of being the only person who has those experiences, feelings, desires. Now that may be particularly true of trans* people and I know it is true of trans* people, but I think it is also true of young gay people, young lesbian

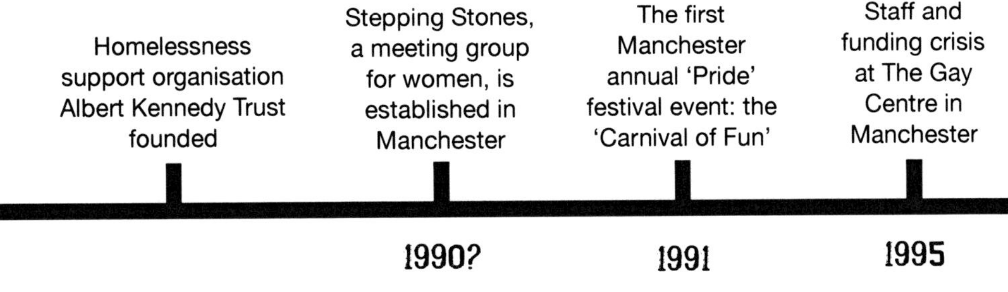

people, young bisexual people. You know that, so that interests me, why is that when things have changed from when I was young, yeah? That that is still the case, so that's a gap, I'd like to understand that more. 'Cause I'd like to think you could get to a point where that wasn't true, you know, where children and young people as well as adults felt okay about growing up gay, yeah. That's right, because maybe you only become aware of your own family really for quite a long time, that's the significant reference point and that might be the reason for what I'm talking about 'cause if most people grow up in families that haven't got gay people in them then maybe it's just going to be, that's what I think the gap is, I want to understand whether it's just kind of inevitable because of what you're saying, 'cause you don't become aware of it.'

While the interviews were largely focused on younger interviewers asking older activists about their experiences, there were of course more conversational moments in the interview, which provide a glimpse of the experiences of current young people. One young woman commented:

'My dad's been a bit of nightmare about it. I know he loves me and he's a great dad, like I really like him. But he always kind of goes, "Why are you still going to that gay group?" and I'm like... No, I read a story and I was like telling him about reading the story and this girl started crying and then he was like, "Who is she?" And I was like, "Oh, she's just someone at this group." And then he was like, "Is she gay?" I was like, It's a group, LGBTQ Young People." He was like, "Well, you going, you're not gay." I'm like, "Yes, I am." He's like, "You just think you are." I'm like, "I sleep with women, have sex with women, this is gay."'

The interviewer, who was 18, reflected:

'But I just find it a bit hard being a teenager like, there's so many social pressures all the time.'

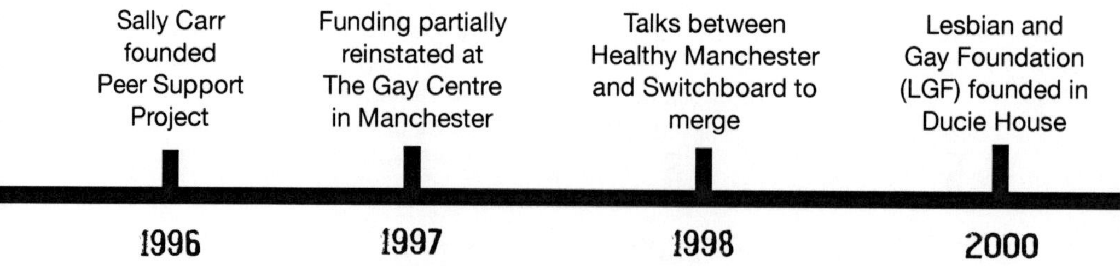

Her 24 year old interviewee, not much older, commented with feeling:

'Yeah. Oh God, I wouldn't be a teenager again if someone paid me. No thank you.'

Maeve Bishop reflected:

'I was thinking "Oh things haven't changed much." 'Cause things have changed massively as well, and my feeling is they've changed loads and they haven't changed at all. So violence against women is still massive. ... Yeah, thing is that are better would be things like the police response to it. So back in the '70s it was really poor.'

'Some guy like properly groped my arse ... But I was like really angry about it and I was like properly angry. And I went to my head of year and was like, "I know his name, I know what year he is, I want him done for sexual harassment or something, or at least excluded." And she went, "Well we'll give him a detention 'cause you're just overreacting. Boys will be boys, you're going to have to face this all the time through your life." ... And my ex-boyfriend punched him in the face and got excluded for two weeks. I was like 14 and so my formative years. "Boys will be boys" that's just awful, I hate that phrase. ... It's like, "No, actually, because when he becomes 18 that's ... It's actually really threatening and actually that's going to turn into assault and like you were actually okaying that sort of treatment of women."'

Growing older can sometimes make a difference. Youth worker Sally Carr reflected on how her experiences of homophobia changed, and life became easier, as she got older:

'My own experiences of homophobia have reduced because I am privileged, you know, I've got into a privileged position where I can drive about in my car and I can work in places that I want to work, so I'm not on the bus, I'm not at school, I'm not in the street, I'm not facing that day to day homophobia that many of the young people that I work with face and I'm very, that's very much

Lesbian Community Project (formerly Lesbian Link) manages the LGBT Centre, Manchester

Manchester City Council's LGBT Staff Group forms, promoting LGBT rights and support staff

Section 28 of the Local Government Act repealed by the Labour government.

2003

in my mind that homophobia still exists but I'm not experiencing it, so that's a significant change for me but still a battle for young people that I've got to be aware of and continue to support those young people to address that. And, you know, I've met people through this journey, I've met doctors and I've met solicitors and I've met politicians, met people who I perhaps would not have otherwise met if I hadn't been in this position. And being able to influence them to make changes that are more accepting of LGBT young people.'

MANCHESTER: SAFE PLACE?

Sometimes in efforts to try and grasp the complicated and uneven changes in the lives of LGBT people, participants struggled with articulating not only change over time, but where change was happening, and where it might not be happening.

The stories in this book are centred on Manchester, a place with a long history of gay rights activism and a large gay community. Many assume that with the move to a gay-friendly city like Manchester, life becomes a lot easier for LGBT people. Liam Mason reflected that while Manchester might be considered a safe area for many LGBT people, the reality could be more complex:

'Manchester, you would have thought would be instantly quite a safe space because of its sort of LGBT history, Canal Street being like known across the country. But actually, I think a lot of people rest on that too much, saying, "Well actually Manchester must be really friendly for LGBT people," but that's the over-generalisation. I think the attitudes are really varied. I think we're slowing changing them, a step at a time. I don't think it's going to be an overnight fix, and certainly in my lifetime attitudes have changed drastically.'

So for some participants, life feels okay now, and ongoing problems with LGBT rights were seen to be an issue in other parts of the world only:

'Yeah, we've seen some dreadful things happen internationally, really horrific

LIK:T Young Women's Health Project begins, as do the annual Young Women's Summer Camps

Civil Partnership Act enables same-sex couples to enter into civil union

LGBT Youth North West sets up as a company and adopts the Peer Support Project.

LGBT History Month begins

2004

2005

things about the videos that came out on YouTube about the young men being hanged in Iran, about people being stoned to death, about some of the African nations taking a more punitive approach and criminalising homosexuality even further with death sentences.'

'We see it much worse in other places, 'cause we've, we've developed in the right direction over the last 30 years, what gay rights politics tends to be involved in now. LGBT politics tends to be involved more internationally now, when you look at the recent laws in Uganda for example. And you look at places like Iran where it's a capital offence, and you're executed, erm, Russia and Belarus where there's a lot of homophobia and lots of right wing thugs beating gay people up, countries like that. Erm, where in those days we didn't look outside our own country because there were, there was enough going on here for us to deal with at the time.'

LGBT Youth North West support the LGBT Community in Russia at Manchester Pride 2013

Many participants mentioned Russia as the interviews happened around the time of the 2014 Winter Olympics in Sochi, when there was much international attention on Russia's harsh stance on LGBT rights:

'It's slightly political, but if you look at the state of Russia for instance at the moment, where they've made it a criminal act to promote LGBT propaganda, it's ludicrous. It is what it is. There are gay people in the world. There are trans* people in the world. I think that's one of the bigger issues. But when you look at places like the UK where it's genuinely not an issue, it's crazy to think that

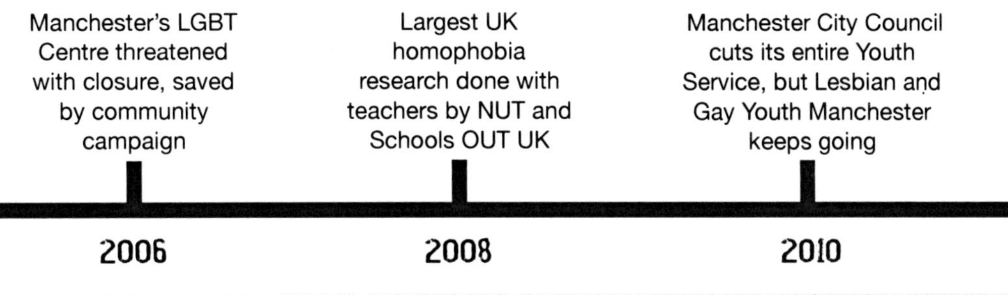

there are places in the world as big as Russia that are making it a criminal offence to promote LGBT rights, so definitely acceptance is the big thing.'

One participant talked about two extremes:

'One extreme, which is some countries of the world, real cruelty, imprisonment, violence towards LGBT people … and the other extreme, real celebrations of progress. So you know, gay marriage and Clare Balding and Sandy Toksvig and Jodie Foster getting married. You know, there's sort of some stories which are great and which are positive and celebrations of equality for LGBT people. So I get those two extremes.'

For others homophobia can create a culture of fear so that threats are identified closer to home. There were several references to the BNP, to the rise in support for UKIP, and sometimes the figure of the 'Islamic Fundamentalist' also appeared. One interviewee told us about a threatening situation he'd been involved in in Manchester:

'They said something extremely threatening and for a split second I thought, "They're going to kill me." Because as a gay man in that sort of situation at night in a dark car park, even for someone as out and as well balanced as I am there was always lurking in the back of your head that someone was going to pull a knife on you. And it was at a time when the knife culture was very prevalent in Manchester. And I turned on my heels, ran back into school and found a member of, probably the only other member of staff who was there and was sort of semi-hysterical for about five minutes. And, strange as it may seem, there are many parts of Manchester I would not go to at night when it was dark with my partner or even on my own because I know I would probably end up with a knife in my back. Those places still exist and in a place, a sort of BNP ripe city like Manchester, er, it's really sad that it still exists.'

Maeve Bishop offered an insightful reflection on the tendency to locate homophobia and threats to gay rights in other countries or places:

'I think there's a lot of chat that's like, "Oh, you shouldn't complain because we've got it so much better than lots of other places." First of all, that's like, "Yeah, maybe in legislation, but not in practice." And second of all, just because you've got it better than someone else doesn't mean that you should stop fighting. I think keep going until you're perfect, which is never, so keep going.'

'Keep going' feels like a perfect articulation of the ethos of the LGBTYNW, which as an organisation is constantly changing and reflecting on its practice.

One participant reflected on how in the early days the Centre was not always understanding of, or listening to young people, but was instead paternalistic:

'The decision [was made] to separate out a parents' group from youth groups, to allow separate spaces for dealing with and discussing issues and if parents had their own issues for example they were better served by setting up a parents' group where they could think about their own issues and not offload that onto younger people.'

It is only a couple of years ago that the 'name games' that begin every youth session in the LGBT Centre began to include, as well as introducing people's names and some detail of their lives, to also include the person's pronoun, in recognition of the importance of being trans* inclusive and creating a space where trans* people could be recognised as they feel comfortable. Such a significant change quickly comes to feel usual, though of course it is hardly (yet) a common practice outside of LGBT-friendly spaces.

As a more recent observation Sally Carr reflected that 'perhaps what we do these days is reach a broader cross section of people and we're also getting people who are further out from living in an urban centre', though this might not always be obvious from the interviews. This book shares some of the stories of LGBT activism from Manchester and beyond, and while there is still much more to reflect upon, learn, discover and celebrate, we would

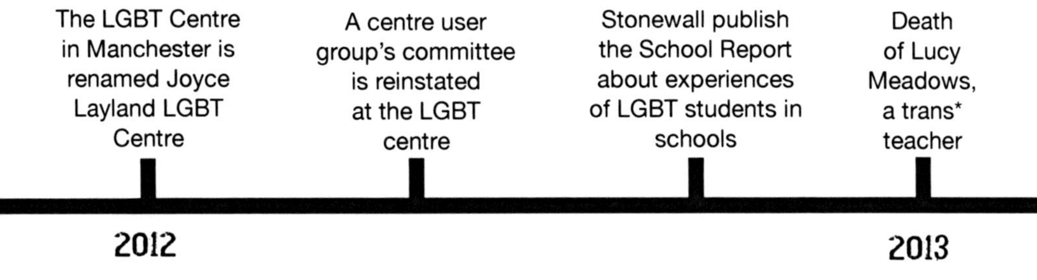

encourage you to consider the ways in which, and the many other people behind, 'How We Got Here'.

'Equal' Marriage Act enables same sex couples to marry

Sidney St Café launched at the Joyce Layland LGBT Centre, Manchester

Library at the LGBT Centre in Manchester renamed Jaye Bloomfield Library

Present day

2013

2015

CHAPTER 2

THIS IS HOW WE GOT HERE:

TRAINING AND INTERVIEWS

LIAM MASON

The 'This is How We Got Here' project carried out by LGBT Youth North West focused on four key areas of LGBT history, these were:

Firstly, the activist community history of LGBT Manchester through the development of one of the UK's first purpose built Gay Centres. This centre, The Joyce Layland LGBT Centre, is active today. The youth group involved in this part of the project access the LGBT Centre at their regular Tuesday and Saturday sessions.

Secondly, the history of Schools OUT UK, the LGBT campaigning organisation that celebrated its 40th anniversary in 2014. Teachers who were sacked when their sexuality was discovered founded this group, and later set up LGBT History Month. This project aimed to hear from activists who have been involved during Schools OUT UK's history and what the personal, community and political impact is of the work they have done. For many of the young people at LGBTYNW, school can be a difficult time, and despite support of organisations like LGBTYNW and Schools OUT UK, homophobia, biphobia and transphobia still exist. The young people aimed to find out how this work started, and what can be done to make school feel safer in the future.

Thirdly, the LGBT activist history of youth work in Manchester. Manchester boasts the second oldest LGBT youth group in the North of England, having been set up by parents of gay teenagers. This project aimed to hear from youth workers, volunteers and young people who have accessed provisions, discovering the history and the impact of youth work on Manchester's LGBT young people.

The project also included a visit to the Glasgow Women's Library by the Young Women's Health Project. The Young Women's Group is run by and for young lesbian and bisexual women aged 12+, and this trip encouraged the young women to think about women, lesbian and bisexual women's activism, particularly focusing on activism, communication, education and empowerment through literature, badges and zines. This trip, and the underrepresentation of women throughout the project, led to the fourth memories day, one specifically for women who had been involved in activism.

This project has been made possible by the Heritage Lottery Fund (HLF). The HLF have funded the This Is How We Got Here project for the youth workers and young people to be able to produce a range of resources including this book, educational lesson plans and drama pieces based on the oral histories interviews (which can be viewed at:www.youtube.com/user/LGBTYouthNorthWest) and a mural created by Hebe Phillips and the young people of LGBT Youth North West, displayed at the Joyce Layland LGBT Centre, Manchester.

As informal educators it is important that the young people could gain numerous skills and experiences from this project, they learned about conducting oral histories and interviewed activists. LGBT Youth North West has the LGBT Youth College, part of the Open College awards scheme. All the young people who took part could complete the newly written module (created for this project) on 'Oral Histories Research Skills'. This is an important outcome from the project.

Some young people's lives can be just as 'wibbly wobbly' as this project became, and as much as the history they were learning about. Gaining educational recognition for their work enables them to access different methods of learning and to open up new opportunities.

HISTORY OF LESBIAN THE LGBT CENTRE

This part of this project was conducted by the young people of Lesbian and Gay Youth Manchester.

The focus: the history of the LGBT Centre where the group is held

The memory day: 1st March 2014

The oral histories training was fun and interactive, to respond to the needs of the young people. While working with the young people as a group we explored what history is, how it affects us and how wibbly wobbly LGBT interconnected history really is.

The young people were given the task of imagining what the future of LGBT Groups could look like in 10 years and what the future of the LGBT Centre could be.

Participants were asked what their ideal - and possibly fantasy future - centre could look like. But how do we get there? How did we get here?

The formulation of interview questions was inspired by investigating the building and speaking to staff. The young people became inquisitive and wanted to know more.

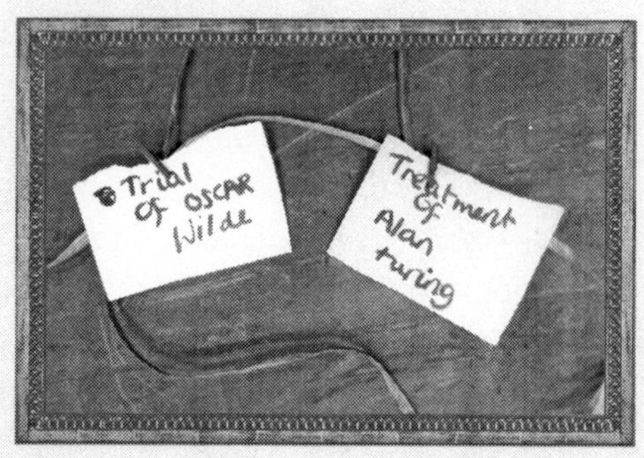

An exercise which showed the crossover of the LGBT community with wider UK events

WHAT WOULD YOUR IDEAL YOUTH CENTRE LOOK LIKE?

During the Memories Day on the 1st March, 14 people who had used or worked in the LGBT Centre came to be interviewed by the young people.

Although many of the young people were nervous for their first interviews they all came out feeling confident and saying they had learned interesting and often unusual facts about LGBT history in Manchester.

This is what one young person said about conducting interviews:

'I was worried that the person I was interviewing would think that I was too cheerful, but I was excited to do more.'

The day ended with a group discussion. The combination of older LGBT Centre users, the young people and members of other groups who use the centre today contrasted and complimented each other. We came full circle, why did we need the centre then to why we still need the centre now?

HISTORY OF LGBT ACTIVISM IN EDUCATION

The second part of the project was conducted by the young people of Wednesdays in Stockport.

The focus: LGBT activism in education

The memory day: 10th and 11th May 2014 - The Schools OUT UK Conference

The young people from the Wednesdays LGBT group in Stockport group jumped whole-heartedly into this project. They researched and learnt a lot. The time-scale was limited in comparison with the Manchester memory day, however, this did not deter the young people from Wednesdays. The way the

Examples of thought processes young people from Stockport had in preparing for the Schools OUT UK event

oral history training was carried out was adapted to fit the learning style of the group.

The young people enjoyed researching LGBT history and presenting back to the rest of the group. The areas the young people researched included Schools OUT UK, Section 28 and what activism is.

Communication became a focal point of the sessions. The young people had to communicate their ideas, questions and responses clearly. Future sessions explored interview technique.

The Wednesdays in Stockport group is a very talented and creative group. Music by LGBT artists was played to allow space for reflection and the creation of their questions.

Can you tell me (more) about your involvement with Schools OUT UK?

Can you tell me about your experiences in schools – as a pupil and/or as a teacher?

Do you think about yourself as an activist?

Do you feel like any of the protests you have been involved in have changed anything?

How do you think teachers can help?

What you think about the current LGBT movement?

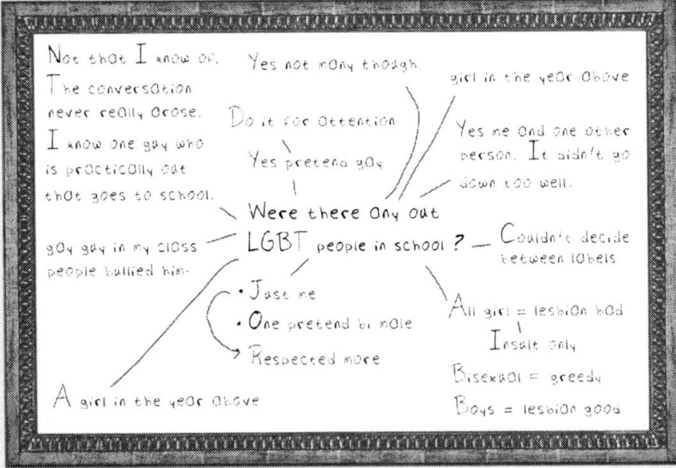

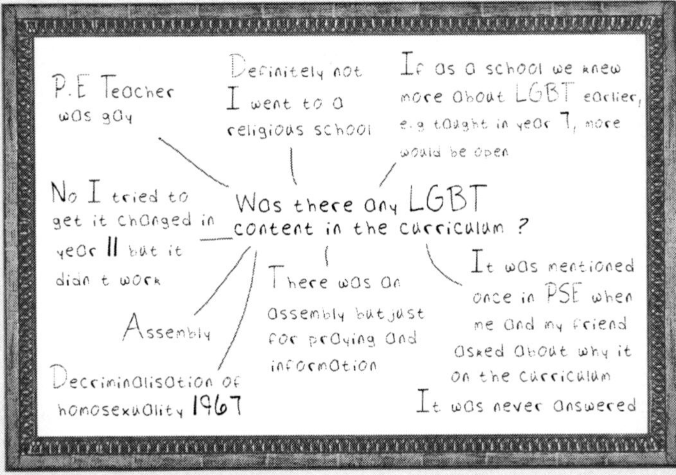

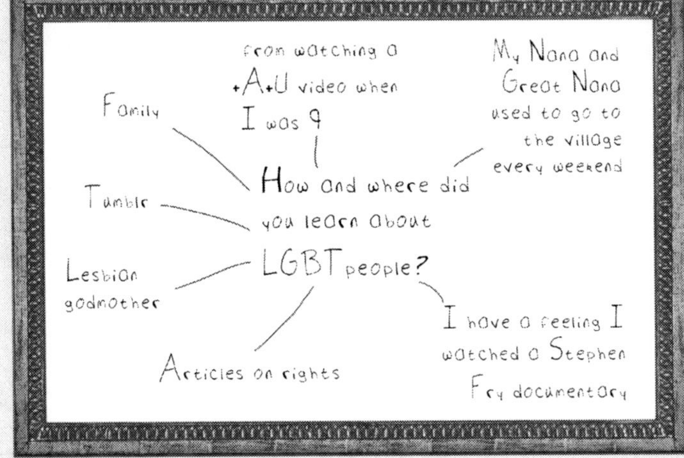

Examples of thought processes young people from Stockport had in preparing for the Schools OUT UK event

THE SCHOOLS OUT UK CONFERENCE

In 2014, Schools OUT UK turned 40, and with over 100 delegates travelling from across the UK and as far as Mexico, there was a lot to reflect on and celebrate.

Schools OUT UK started as the Gay Teachers' Group after John Warburton was sacked from his school and banned from working for the Inner London Education Authority (ILEA) for telling the truth. Some students in his class had seen him coming out of a gay bar and they asked him if he was gay. He said that he was. That was enough to finish his teaching career in London.

Sue Sanders, chair of the organisation, opened the event saying:

'Since 1974, we have been on an amazing journey, from teachers being sacked for being gay in the 1970s to the present day where the law recognises equality. The challenge is to translate the law into reality, given that teachers are still not receiving compulsory equality and diversity training unlike staff in other sectors, such as criminal justice.'

Tony Fenwick, CEO of Schools OUT UK stated his ongoing concerns:

'We live in a society where I can marry my same sex partner but I still cannot walk down the street holding his hand without receiving abuse. We are here today to celebrate the progress that has been made but more must be done to challenge prejudice.'

It appeared that many people on the day were inspired, and it was an opportunity to share experiences from both a personal level and a societal one, as Amelia Lee, a youth worker, reflects:

'The highlight for me has been hearing from the people who 20, 30 and even 40 years ago were breaking new ground by being visible and outspoken. They didn't believe some things were possible that we have now. Their energy was inspirational to the young people and educators at the conference.'

Lena Milosovic is a teacher who came out at the National Union of Teachers (NUT) conference in 1988 whilst speaking on a motion against Section 28. She said:

A number of young people from Stockport opening the Schools OUT UK Conference 2014, alongside members of the Schools OUT UK Committee

Schools OUT UK book authors, Alan Jackson, Tim Lucas, Geoff Hardy and Peter Bradley interviewed by Julie Bremner

Members of the Schools OUT UK Committee with the birthday cake made by Sidney Street Café

Lena Milosevic describing her experience of coming out at the NUT Conference

'Sadly some issues are still relevant today and this is why this work has to continue.'

This highlighted the 'wibbly wobbly' nature of LGBT activism, with some people, schools, organisations and communities still unable to benefit from changes in law and attitude.

The day included key note speakers, workshops and opportunities to network, as well as the chance to be interviewed by young people.

These young people reflected on the conference and the interview experience:

'I listened to Lena speak in the main conference and I wanted to know more.'

'They were amazing, they have had so many different experiences.'

'I was nervous going into my first interview, but I had someone with me so it made it easier.'

'The experience was amazing, I loved the atmosphere.'

Jak West reflected on meeting activists who he believes helped his own educational experiences:

'This was so interesting, the people who we interviewed today have made school a safer place for so many. Had they not stood up to Section 28, come out in their schools as students and teachers, fought for their and others' rights, who knows what school might have been like for me?'

YOUTH WORKERS AND WOMEN IN ACTIVISM EVENTS

These events were the led by the young people of WYnotLGBTQ in Wythenshawe. A number of young people who had already been trained in oral histories were involved and this led to a high level of peer learning, and sharing of experiences, as well as development of learning about activism.

The focus: LGBT activism in youth work

The memory day: 28th June 2014

The training focused heavily on exploration of what youth work meant to the young people, their experiences of youth work projects and interactions with youth workers.

'Youth workers make us feel comfortable, create a safe space, support us and are there for us.'

'From the youth groups we feel accepted, and we are educated in different things from school that we really need, we meet different people and friends.'

'Experiences we remember included Pride, Pink Box, sports, IDAHOBIT.'

Pride refers to Manchester Pride that LGBT Youth North West takes part in every year. Pink Box is a North West regional LGBT showcase and competition held in May to coincide with International Day Against Homophobia, Biphobia and Transphobia (IDAHOBIT).

'Youth work helps us feel more confident, [it is a] supportive environment. We can be ourselves, whereas at home some of us can't be ourselves and relaxed. It has inspired us. [The] friendly youth workers are

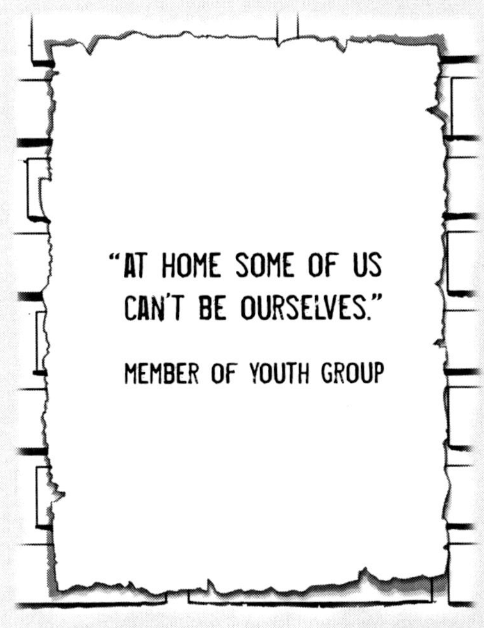

Glasgow Women's Library entrance

informal and cool here which is great, it helps you become more relaxed and participate more comfortably.'

This was the starting point to developing questions, and to help the young people reflect on how LGBT youth work may have changed over the years. Some of the young people involved had taken part in the other memory days. They imparted some of their experiences and knowledge. This peer education- the learning from each other and discussing commonality gave this day a very different atmosphere to the other sessions. The training for this event was done in an intensive day. There are benefits to carrying out this type of oral histories training in a day. Young people become more focused and it becomes all they think about for that period of time.

This memories day invited youth workers from across the region to attend, be interviewed and share their stories and experiences. Eight youth workers were interviewed and one past member of the group attended, speaking about how youth work, specifically LGBT youth work, impacted upon their life.

Young people's reflections after doing interviews included:

'People have very different experiences of youth work but can also share lots of similarities.'

'My highlight was hearing the interviewees favourite things about youth work.'

Finally, and importantly, there was the Women in Activism memory day.

This day had been inspired by the trip to the Glasgow Women's Library, where the Young Women's Health Project had the opportunity to visit the archives, learning specifically about women's history, lives, achievements and activism.

On this trip, the young women and staff were able to learn and participate in a number of dynamic and engaging ways, studying books, comics, zines, badges and artwork whilst developing new skills and knowledge in these areas.

Zines, magazines and badges shared with the Young Women's Health Project in Glasgow Women's Library

The visit to the Glasgow Women's Library highlighted the need for women's representation and the current lack of representation and inclusion of information in mainstream libraries that focuses on women's historical and cultural contributions to activism and society. The project aimed to ensure that this would not happen with the oral history interviews, so included a fourth event for the interviews, a specific 'Women in Activism' day.

Having trained as oral historians for a number of the other events, a number of the young women attended the final memories day on the 29th June 2014 at the Joyce Layland LGBT Centre. These young women interviewed women who are activists in the community, have been involved in the LGBT Centre, Schools OUT UK and LGBT youth work, so there was a lot to talk about!

One young woman reflected on her interview saying she had learnt a lot about modern feminism and I heard some interesting stories about how difficult it is to be involved in activism.

The core of the sessions

Throughout all of the vastly differently delivered the oral history sessions, a number of core themes were covered. These themes were the foundation of the oral histories research as a method. Young people explored what makes a good interview, how to ask questions and what makes a relevant question. Active listening skills were developed and improved with each interview that a young person did. Sharing the experiences of being interviewed was invaluable for the young people as it enabled them to understand the importance of being clear in an interview. While many of the young people felt nervous, the support from peers, and those who were being interviewed enabled them to conduct the excellent interviews which you will read throughout this book.

Ethics and consent

All the young people had a very good understanding about ethical considerations and the reasoning behind the need for consent. The young people were able to discuss what could make them, and the person being interviewed, feel uncomfortable during an interview. The main ethical problem that came up during group discussions was the use of language and how that can affect the way the interview can proceed. As the young people were being trained as oral historians who were often asking about personal stories they had to ensure that the interviewee agreed to and understood how their interviews would be used and shared.

Ethics is a crucial part of oral histories research, and after conversations about ethics, the young people felt confident in knowing what to do in a difficult interview. As one of the young people, who later grew in confidence, stated:

'At first I was unsure of the best ways to deal with responses to questions that I didn't agree with.'

FROM THOUGHTS TO PAPER

Following all the events, the team were left with 45 interviews and hundreds of hours of stories to share in this book. So how did that happen?

Transcriptions of the interviews were produced, capturing hundreds of pages of interviews. Young people had created and asked questions which highlighted particular themes and areas of activism. These themes were "coded" using the Technology of Participation Workshop Consensus Method. These key themes were selected: the Joyce Layland LGBT Centre, education, youth work, coming out, women's work, difficulties, allies, friends, families, activism, policies, and changes in government. These themes enabled the team to define chapters.

Authors for chapters were recruited, with the authors having a particular interest or experience in that area of activism. Having worked with the young people from the project, and reading the relevant transcriptions, authors were able to select particular quotes and statements, writing chapters based on stories activists had shared. The team met and communicated regularly, and often young people were consulted by individual authors to ensure accessibility, and to clarify that they had accurately written what the young people had heard from the interviewees.

The information shared in this book came directly from the young people and those they interviewed. The young people, alongside the activists, were integral to this project. You are invited to remember, reflect on and discover 'How We Got Here' throughout this book.

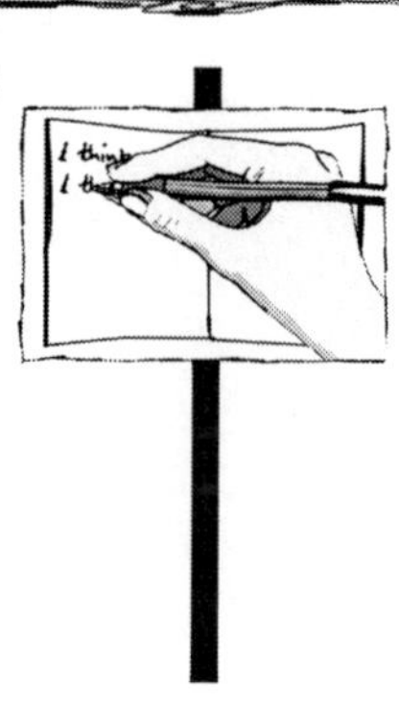

This activity is to help you consider how you communicate with other people and what you might tell them. We used this activity to train peer researchers.

Firstly think of five different people you talk to such as teacher, friends, parents…

Then think about how you talk to them.
Do you joke? Do you use slang?
Do you use full sentences?

Then think about how much you tell them about what you did yesterday.

Who are you talking to?	How do you talk to them?	What do you tell them?
Friend	I have jokes and talk informally	I tell them the details of my day

Overall, this section of the project was incredibly valuable for the young people, staff, and the activists who were involved. It will ensure that there is a legacy and understanding of what LGBT activism looked like, and how the young people who interviewed and were educated through the project have become activists themselves.

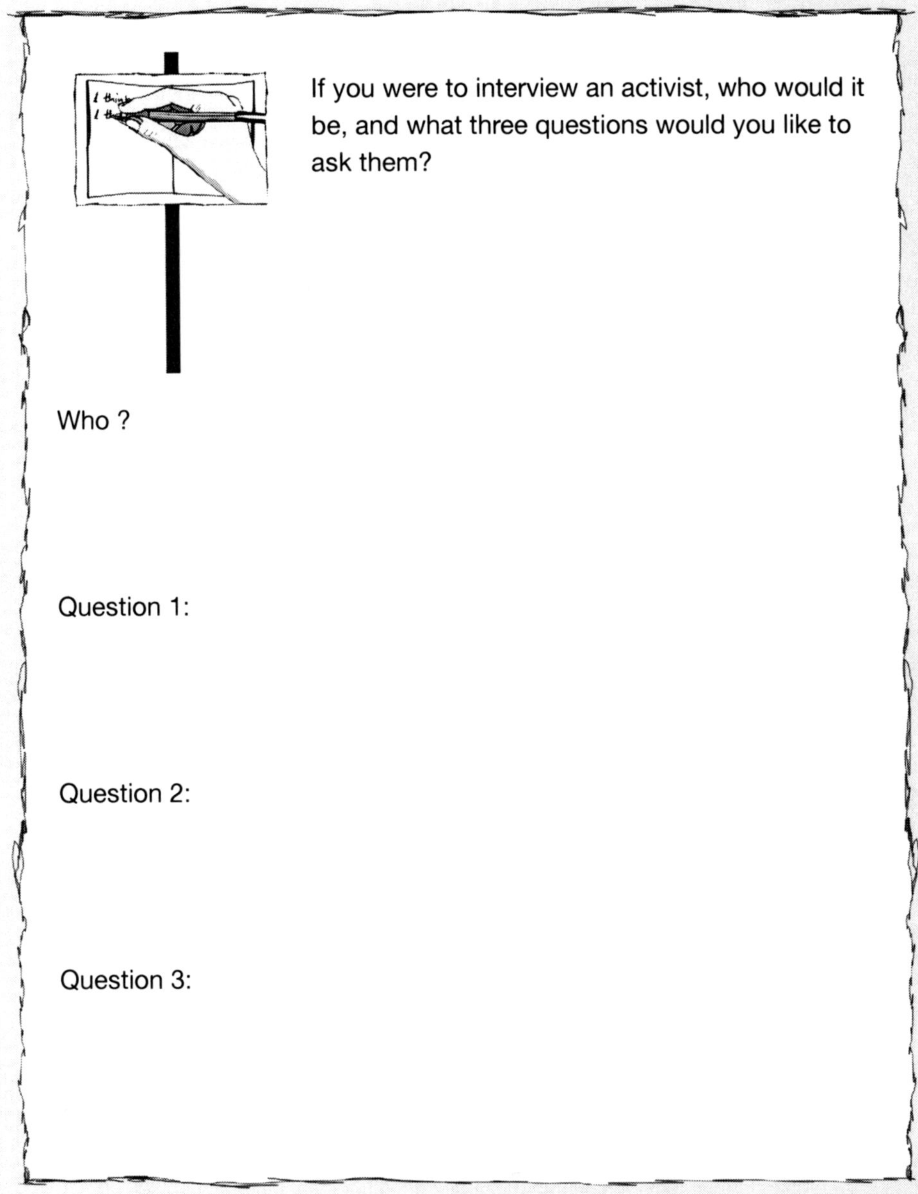

If you were to interview an activist, who would it be, and what three questions would you like to ask them?

Who ?

Question 1:

Question 2:

Question 3:

CHAPTER 3

UNDER THE MICROSCOPE

GOVERNMENT POLITICS AND THE MEDICALISATION OF LGBT LIVES

NIAMH MOORE

Leslie Feinberg, a self-portrait from their own collection, www.transgenderwarrior.org

This chapter was written as the news came in that Leslie Feinberg, transgender warrior and author of *Stone Butch Blues* has died, on 15 November 2014, age 65 of complications from multiple tick-borne illnesses including Lyme's disease. Failure to get appropriate medical attention and adequate diagnosis is part of the story of Feinberg's life, death and many years of illness. Prejudice against her transgender identity, as well as lack of knowledge of tick-borne diseases, contributed to many years of ill-health. Similarly, the setting up of a Gay Centre, at a time of collective activism and a sympathetic Labour Council in Manchester, shows a glimpse of the difference that government and medicine can make to how LGBT lives are lived.

Manchester Lesbian and Gay Chorus, thanks to MLGC Online

At the same time, while this book project emerged out of the ongoing success of the Gay Centre, now the Joyce Layland LGBT Centre, this chapter was also written as two young gay men in Manchester were brutally beaten for singing songs from the musical *Wicked* on a tram. This horrific event was followed by a coming together of Manchester's Lesbian and Gay Chorus (MLGC) as well as a host of non-LGBT specific choirs and singing groups. These included the Hallé choir and choirs from Stockport and beyond to insist collectively that it should be '#Safe To Sing' on the tram and in Piccadilly Gardens, Manchester.

With hundreds turning out to sing songs on the tram and share rainbow-coloured cupcakes announcing 'cake not hate', as a political message rather than a nostalgic version of femininity, this is evidence of how the LGBT community and allies deal with ongoing homophobic violence. Such is the complicated world which LGBT people inhabit.

Cake Not Hate, thanks to MLGC Online

This chapter draws on interviews to discuss both government policies and medicalisation of LGBT lives. These are two key, and related, issues affecting many LGBT people. This chapter focuses specifically on the issues that were raised in interviews, so there is also much that the chapter does not cover, but that can be read about elsewhere. There is not much here about HIV/AIDS, though of course ample written elsewhere on HIV/AIDS; and there is a separate chapter on Section 28 legislation. Issues raised here, such as life before the decriminalization of homosexual sex; the transformations wrought by the introduction of civil partnership and marriage; the Gender Recognition Act; all these certainly recur throughout this book.

The Wolfenden Report, published in 1957 in the UK, recommended that "homosexual behaviour between consenting adults in private should no longer be a criminal offence". This was a significant change from prevailing medical and legal practice at the time, where homosexual behaviour was often understood as a disease or a sign of deviance. Often called the Wolfenden Report after Lord Wolfenden, the chairman of the committee, its full title is the *Report of the Departmental Committee on Homosexual Offences and Prostitution*. The recommendations in the report eventually led to the passage of the *Sexual Offences Act 1967 (England and Wales only*) ten years after the report was originally published.

The Decriminalization of Homosexual Sex

The Sexual Offences Act 1967 (England and Wales only) decriminalised homosexual acts in private between two men over the age of 21. The act did not apply to the Navy or the Armed Forces – where LGBT people were not allowed to serve openly until 2000. Homosexuality was decriminalised in Scotland in 1980 and in Northern Ireland in 1982.

The Age of Consent

The age of consent for homosexual sex between two men was 21 in 1967, whereas it was then 16 for heterosexuals. There was no age of consent for lesbians. The age of consent for gay sex was reduced to 18 in 1994; an equal age of consent finally became law in January 2001, so the age of consent is now 16 across the UK, regardless of the genders of the people involved.

DECRIMINALISING SEX BETWEEN MEN

Janet Batsleer was scathing about what she saw as the stupidity of some of these laws:

'And what it was like! You don't get that now so much really, this kind of stuff, stupid laws. A bloke can have sex with a girl when he's 16 but if he's gay he can't have sex with his boyfriend until he's 21. Well he can now. ... This is stupid because they're both sex, just different kinds.'

Sue Sanders remembered the Wolfenden Report:

'I can remember when the Wolfenden Report came out, which was in '67. So how old am I? I'll tell you what the Wolfenden Report is because it's important to know. The Wolfenden Report was the report that said, and it came out in '57, and it had been set up to find out whether homosexuality should be criminalised and how to deal with prostitution. And it was very interesting that they put the two together. So it was looking at the whole issue of how governments dealt with prostitution and how governments dealt with homosexuality. And in 1957... they had this little committee of people, and Wolfenden was the head of it, and it was all male except for the secretary. And he was terribly embarrassed about the words homosexuality and prostitution, talking about this in front of a woman, who was the secretary who was writing everything down. So he looked at a plate of biscuits that were in front of him and he said, "Okay, it's Huntleys & Palmers." It's a brand of biscuits called Huntleys & Palmers. So Huntleys were homosexuals and Palmers were prostitutes. That's the culture that we're talking about. This was a man who was embarrassed about using the words homosexuality and prostitution in mixed company and it was his job to decide what the government should do around homosexuality and prostitution. So he came out in '57, the committee came out in favour of decriminalising homosexuality, in '57. It wasn't until 1967, ten years later, that we get the

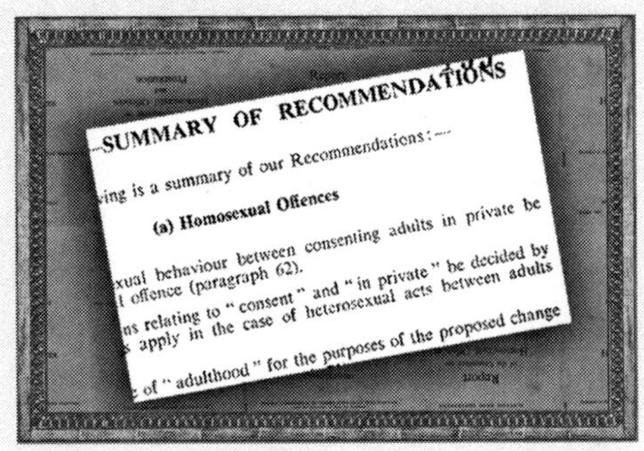
SUMMARY OF RECOMMENDATIONS

...ving is a summary of our Recommendations:—

(a) Homosexual Offences

...xual behaviour between consenting adults in private be
...l offence (paragraph 62).
...ns relating to "consent" and "in private" be decided by
... apply in the case of heterosexual acts between adults
...of "adulthood" for the purposes of the proposed change

Wolfenden Report summary, Manchester Archives

law which says it's legal if it's consenting, if you're over 21 and if it's in private. The irony is, more men got arrested post '67 as they tried to work out what was private.'

As Sue indicated, the Wolfenden Report specifically referred to homosexual behaviour in private, which left homosexual sex in public places still an offence. Brian Jacobs discussed the impact of being arrested for cottaging – having sex with another consenting man in public toilets (which were often built to resemble cottages) – as well as the common practice of entrapment by the police:

'One of the most bizarre episodes in my life was being arrested by a pretty policeman, you won't know this, but until quite recently pretty policemen were employed by police forces to arrest gay men who were cottaging. You know about cottaging? And I mean that goes right back to the 1950s when there were some really historic cases where important people were arrested and sent to jail under the then law. And it was only in 1967 when I became legal and before 1967 I had been committing illegal acts, erm, and was very aware that I was a potential criminal I mean which used to really, well it didn't upset me it just made me very angry that prior to 1967 when I was aged 22 I was a criminal. And in the '80s I was actually arrested by a pretty policeman, a very pretty policeman, exceedingly pretty, exceedingly handsome encased in leather who was there…And it was sanctioned by the Home Office. … This wasn't an aberration with any particular police force this was actually encouraged and aided and abetted by the then Home Secretary and it didn't actually formally end until, I probably haven't got the dates right, but I think late '90s after Tony Blair had become Prime Minister. And I was arrested, erm, and I was a lawyer so here I find myself being arrested facing a trial and, cutting a long story very short, I decided I wasn't going to, they wanted me, they wanted me obviously to plead guilty because that's what they did and for me to, which would have ended my professional career because you weren't allowed to, if you were in a court and been declared guilty on any count you had to stop being a solicitor, you'd be taken off the roll of solicitors. So, but from two points of view, from a personal point of view which was more important than the professional point of view, I was determined to fight this and, cutting a long story short, I fought this and it's so long ago I can't even remember the details now but the outcome was because I stood really strongly on the, on my innocence the court was forced to drop the charges.

And I'd like to think… that case in which I was involved eventually led to the Home Office realising they were walking down the wrong path and eventually led to the Home, the then Home Secretary, whenever it was in the late '90s, saying, "This has to stop," and it did stop. So another episode of me challenging the establishment. I mean it was, I mean looking back I now think I must have been mad. I mean I must have been mad finding myself in that situation to start with, but, you know, I was, I was a [laughs], I was a fully operating sexual being and if I couldn't, you know, this was the '80s and it happened but I wasn't going to let the establishment get me. So another, another incident where, another episode of where I challenged.'

Maeve Bishop also offered some reflections on the perverse sexism of much legislation:

'But I always think with those kinds of rules that they're really sexist because sodomy is illegal, like women's sexuality just doesn't matter.'

And how shocking some of the (lack of) legislation now appears:

'I think it's actually amazing though that, like, on the plus side it's cool that it's changed so much that we find that shocking. 'Cause I know that, for example in England it wasn't illegal to rape your wife until 1993 or 1992, and it's just like I can't imagine a world where that will be considered fine. Like well, we live in one where it's considered fine, do you know what I mean, implicitly, but I can't imagine a world where that's explicitly the law. … I was born then; I was alive, so it's weird.'

As well as these changes in legislation, a further significant change was the removal of homosexuality from the *Diagnostic and Statistical Manual of Mental Disorders*. The shift away from the stigma of a mental health disorder contributed to the long slow process of 'normalising' homosexuality.

MEDICALISATION

The Diagnostic and Statistical Manual of Mental Disorders (DSM).

In 1973 the American Psychiatric Association removed homosexuality from the Diagnostic and Statistical Manual of Mental Disorders (DSM), finally ending the classification of homosexuality as a clinical mental disorder or disease.

Against the assumption of the DSM that homosexuality was some kind of mental illness, the interviews remind us that many mental health issues were more likely to be a result of society's homophobia. John Vincent revealed panic attacks and agoraphobia as consequences of homophobic bullying:

'I was being bullied and I was kind of scared of things, I started being frightened of going out, so I became quite agoraphobic. And I started having panic attacks. And so I got referred by my GP to a counselling group for some sort of therapy, which actually [laughs], kind of, there's an irony in this. The therapy didn't really do much at all, I found it really not very helpful, but the idea that I could actually start saying who I was, was helpful. The therapy didn't actually have much to do with it, it was the fact that I read lots of stuff suddenly, and I was actually talking to people, not in the therapy group, but people generally.'

And while he didn't find therapy helpful, reading and talking to people helped him to feel better.

Brian Jacobs, a teacher and activist, located his nervous breakdown in the context of living through the punitive Thatcher years, as well as in his own personal life of losing a partner, of no longer enjoying his work as a lawyer – and of turning to a busy social life in London:

'We were having to deal with the Thatcher years, the Tory government which was, which was no longer a Thatcher government but was still very repressive.

And all these things accumulated and as a gay out man, a gay man who had lost his partner, erm, and a gay man who was no longer happy in his professional work as a lawyer. … I was also going to London in the mid '90s, I was going to London every weekend and doing outrageous things in London. It was all too much. So I had a nervous breakdown. Quickly recovered, er, and then, erm, with a change in politics in the country, which changed the whole atmosphere of British culture, the fact that so many terrible things were rectified, I mean like male rape, like civil partnerships and of course by that time I'd already met my then partner in '97.'

A change of government, and a change in the legal situation which impacted on many LGBT lives is also what made a difference in his life.

The Gender Recognition Act 2004

The Gender Recognition Act 2004 allows a person to legally change their gender.

Ten years after the introduction of the Gender Recognition Act, Liam Mason is employed as a trans*-specific youth worker, working with the statutory health services:

'I'll also be doing work around a young trans* care pathway for the North West, and that's working with young trans* people's GP. This is in the Young People's Advisory Service once a week as part of a wider project called GP Champs. Again, it's funded by CAMHS. It provides that re-education and information to general practitioners about what they should be doing for trans* people. So even though it's for under 18s that I'll be working with, it will actually have a knock on effect for over 18s as well in terms of trans* healthcare. And various other bits of work with the National Trans* Youth network as well, which is a network of 30 LGBT and trans* groups across the country, to really put trans* awareness on the front foot again and really push it forward.'

In November 2014, the National Trans* Youth Network hosted the first Youth Conference, which 120 trans* young people attended in Manchester- the largest gathering of trans* youth in UK history.

Together these stories provide a glimpse into the ways in which legislation and a prevailing homophobic attitude had severe consequences for many people's health. Changes in legislation, coupled with more public and popular acceptance of LGBT people, plus the ability to talk and meet others is what has helped many LGBT people live less distressing lives.

CIVIL PARTNERSHIP AND GAY MARRIAGE

LGBT Civil Partnership and Marriage

Civil Partnership for same-sex couples, including where a partner has changed gender, has been possible in the UK since the *Civil Partnership Act 2004 (UK).* Marriage for same-sex couples, including where one partner has changed gender, has been possible since 13 March 2014, following the *Marriage (Same Sex Couples) Act 2013*.

Brian Jacobs reflected on the complexity of civil partnership and gay marriage – mulling over the dilemma faced if civil partnerships are automatically converted to marriages, and of the possibilities of extending civil partnership to all couples, including heterosexual couples:

'There is talk that if you are currently civilly partnered that will be transmuted, or whatever the word is, to a marriage so we, actually we could find ourselves being married by the law. We were laughing about this the other night because it would be absolutely hysterical if that actually happened, we wouldn't object but it would be ironic for the two of us to find ourselves married. Some people think that civil partners should be abolished unless it's extended to everybody and I have a certain sympathy for that ... . We want choice as gay people. Why shouldn't non-gay people have the choice to be married or civilly partnered?'

Oliver Bliss' Equality Quilt: 254 hexagons with messages to the 254 MPs that voted against Same Sex Marriage displayed at the People's History Museum, Manchester

PROGRESS? FOR WHOM AND WHERE

With these legislative and other changes, it would be easy to assume that life is now not so difficult in the UK for LGBTQ people. Maeve Bishop, who works in the Sidney Street Community Café at the LGBT Centre in Manchester, reminded us of the ongoing challenges:

'LGBTQ rights are being like picked up by the Government as, like, this weird tool. Like they're [the UK Government] not LGBTQ inclusive at all. But they're like, "Oh, look at us, we're so inclusive 'cause we've got marriage," and they're kind of using it to other nations. … they use[d] women's rights as like an excuse to go and like, I don't know, like in Iraq and Afghanistan, they're like, "Oh, we've got to attack them because they're damaging women's rights." It's like, "Oh, have you seen women's rights in your own place?" … And it's also like well we're absolutely sending LGBTQ people who are trying to claim asylum back to their death, torture or whatever, do you know what I mean? So it's just, [you] need to sort out in your own yard before you can make comments.'

These are timely reflections as, in April 2014, Home Secretary Teresa May announced a review of the handling of asylum claims on the basis of sexuality, after being given reports and research which revealed extensive intrusive questioning of LGBT asylum seekers in which they were asked to 'prove'their sexuality.

Late in the summer of 2014 the Lesbian Immigration Support Group (LISG) moved into an office in the Joyce Layland LGBT Centre, acquiring a dedicated space to continue its work supporting lesbian and bisexual women asylum seekers.

CHANGING ACTIVISM

Youth worker Amelia Lee offered a broad reflection on her observations of how activism has changed over time, from the Lesbian Avengers abseiling on parliament to protest Section 28, to the corporate campaigning of Stonewall. In the process, Amelia captures how activism both tries to drive change and is also responsive to the changing political landscape:

'When I first started getting involved, like I said, 2001, was also still when Section 28 was in, so people weren't allowed to talk about LGBT stuff in school really. I mean that's essentially what that law said. And so there was a need for some of the more radical campaigning, so there was people like the Lesbian Avengers who abseiled into the House of Lords, hijacked a London bus and painted it pink, did quite radical direct action stuff, right?'

'And there is still a place for a lot of that I think, and for some people that's the right way for them to be activists. But if you look at, even from 2001 to now, so that's 13 years, legally there isn't a lot that LGB and T people don't have that heterosexual and non-trans*gendered people have. So in the law books we're relatively equal. In society we're not, there'll be a lag time. I do believe things will change and get better but I think because we've got a lot of law changes, other organisations have had to change. So if you look at somewhere like Stonewall, it wasn't the most radical campaigning place, it was campaigning, but Outrage was the more campaigning group. But Stonewall has become a lot more professional, a lot more corporate. So instead of going out there and protesting it runs a scheme for employers where they have to fill in a self-assessment to see if they can become a Stonewall Champion, so are they really inclusive of LGBT people? And that's a million miles away from protesting on the street but what they've done is created something that people want to be a part of. Companies like to say, "On the Stonewall Index, we're in the top ten." It's started to mean something to places that would have put two fingers up to LGBT people 40 years ago. So they've been quite canny in the way that they've conducted a very gentle corporate change. And I think we've got to look at some subtle ways of changing the culture now that we've got the laws that back that up. So that means that there needs to be a new generation of people thinking about how to make that happen 'cause I don't know, 'cause in a way some of my campaigning years are behind me and some of my campaigning now is going to take place in a different way so we need as many different voices as possible I think to campaign.'

London bus painted pink in protest of Section 28, courtesy of Pink News

CHAPTER 4

SECTION 28:

SECTION TWENTYHATE

TONY FENWICK

Section 28, sometimes referred to as Clause 28, formed part of the *Local Government Act 1988*. Section 28 of that act stated:

(1) A local authority shall not:

(a) intentionally promote homosexuality or publish material with the intention of promoting homosexuality

(b) promote the teaching in any maintained school of the acceptability of homosexuality as a pretended family relationship

Section 28 was only ever used once in court (in an unsuccessful case brought by the Christian Institute against a council that was funding AIDS support). It was finally repealed (taken out of law) in 2003.

While many found that Section 28 proved impracticable to implement as a piece of legislation, at the same time the Act had enormous symbolic significance. First, the use of the word 'promote' made it explicit that 'homosexuality' was considered by the state to be inferior to heterosexuality. Second, a family based on a homosexual relationship was understood as 'pretend'. Third, the act made it clear that it would be wrong to teach that even such a 'pretend' family was 'acceptable'.

However, it wasn't simply the insulting nature of the clause that made it so wrong. It denied local authorities – and by association schools – the right to do their job and to 'promote' equal opportunities where it mattered most, with young people.

Consequently, it united those working in schools as a movement to seek its repeal. It could be argued, that, perhaps paradoxically, this piece of legislation united lesbian and gay teachers and actually generated a strong community committed to change. This chapter examines the impact of Section 28 or 'the clause' locally and nationally through stories from people who were there at the time.

The section began as a private members bill introduced in 1986 by the Earl of Halsbury entitled, ('An Act to restrain local authorities from promoting homosexuality'.) Sue Sanders, a teacher at the time and now chair of LGBT History Month, recollected this moment:

'Hallsbury comes up with his extraordinary statement, which is, 'Over the decades past we have...' What is it? 'Acknowledged or attempted to tackle the oppression of so called minorities. We tackled racism and we got inverted racism.' Anyway, alarm bells ring. He ends his thing with, 'They will push us off the pavement if they give us half a chance,' which really indicates his fear. You know, 'us' is the white men, white heterosexual men. So 'they'll' push 'us' off the pavement because the blacks and the gays want the whole pavement.'

Brian Jacobs, also a teacher, had an ally in government, and he sought to engage directly with those with the power to stop Section 28:

'I had gone to school with Edwina Curry; we used to go Scottish country dancing with each other when we were six. Being Jewish I wrote to the Archbishop, the Chief Rabbi, the Chief Rabbi of the UK. I wrote to a whole host of other people who I thought were important in parliament and out of parliament and I got replies from everybody. I wrote to all the leaders of the then political parties.'

These were not necessarily supportive replies. Brian reflected on the different responses he got, including one letter from Prime Minister Margaret Thatcher:

'She wrote the longest letter and it was a sort of two page defence of Section 28. I mean beautifully written, wonderfully articulate and if I had been an undecided voter in the subject I might have been convinced by the arguments. Needless to say I wasn't. I wrote to her on many different occasions about many different subjects and I would always get a brilliant letter back.'

Brian was considerably less impressed with the replies from the religious leaders:

'The Archbishop of Canterbury wrote a very predictable letter about how homosexuality is a sin blah, blah, blah, blah. The Chief Rabbi interestingly wrote back to me he said 'well I don't know why you're writing to me. We don't have, Jews don't, there are no Jewish homosexuals' which was rather amusing considering that I had introduced myself as a Jew in my letter, but this was an ancient Chief Rabbi who was just about to retire. The succeeding Chief Rabbi of the United Kingdom had rather a different opinion about sexuality, but that's another story.'

So the Lords, the Government and the religious leaders at the time were all in favour of Section 28.

THE ROLE OF THE MEDIA

The press played the role of sensationalising homosexual relationships, Brian explains again:

'Well what started it off was there was outrage, there was outrage in the [home] counties… when this book was produced. … It was a sort of comic book and it featured a family – a so called family, two men and a child, and people were just horrified that two men and a child could be called a family. And it's obviously a lot more complicated than that. This story book … was just one of many books that they printed to reflect how life was in Britain 1980, whatever it was.'

The book in question – Jenny Lives with Eric and Martin – was about a girl with two dads who had a nasty experience in the street when a neighbour made disparaging remarks about their family set up. The graphics – which were photographs not cartoons – featured the little girl having breakfast in bed (on a Saturday when she was bored) with her two dads who were naked from the waist up. These black and white photos were selectively

Jenny Lives with Eric and Martin, Susanne Bösche, 1981

chosen and reproduced in some newspapers as evidence of some kind of depravity with a little girl who was romping on a bed with two grown men who were apparently nude. A campaign to censor what children were being taught was mounted in the media.

Lena Milosevic, a teacher at the time, who came out very publicly at the National Union of Teachers' Conference in her anti-Section 28 protest speech, reflected on the lengths to which the press went to in their obsession with homosexuality. Her account reminds us that even before mobile phone hacking the press had ways and means of invading our privacy:

'The worst criticism and the worst sort of experiences came from the press, for sure. They were just downright nasty and did things that I think are unacceptable, like coming to your house, talking to your neighbours, "What she's like?" you know; talking to your neighbours. I think that complete invasion of privacy that we read about today [was happening then] and I think they still behave badly. And I am pleased to see some exposure of that malpractice. You know, there should be a clear code of conduct for the press as to what line you can go to and I think we are recently- very, very, very recently- with the Leveson enquiry and so on, starting to draw up those lines.'

Many of the people interviewed in the project, like Brian Jacobs, were keen to stress that the law "was never effective and was never aimed at teachers." Tim Lucas, an NUT executive member and a campaigner with Schools OUT UK, stressed the fact that Section 28 targeted local authorities rather than schools:

'In reality it didn't apply to schools, it applied to local government, and schools who didn't want to talk about LGBT issues just used it as an excuse in my view. There was nothing to prevent them doing anything they wanted to. It was the local authority that was in the frame and could not promote itself. I think if any school had wished, and I don't know of any that did, but if any school had wished to support its LGBT students I think it could've done. It could've argued if necessary on the basis of human rights and gone all the way to the United Nations Charter if they needed to defend themselves. It was all based on fear that everyone knew what the press would do to you if you didn't conform. So it really was pernicious in that way.'

Peter Bradley, a retired teacher, talked about the 'stupidity' of the wording:

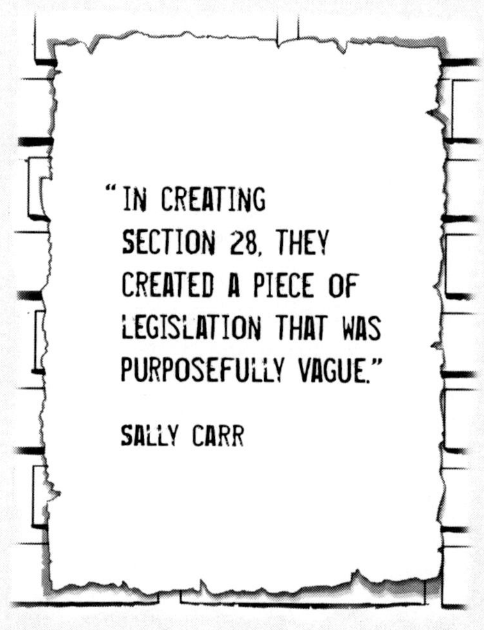

'If you are telling people about the gross domestic product of Brazil, you're not promoting Brazil, you're telling them facts about the country. If you tell people about lesbianism, you're not promoting 'lesbian', so actually, had anyone tested the law?'

Peter added:

'So as a law actually it was ineffective but as a bogie to frighten lesbian and gay, bisexual and transgender, the effect it had was baleful. It frightened people. It made teachers cautious, whether they were gay or not.'

Sally Carr, a youth worker, also commented on the ambiguity of its terminology:

'It was phenomenal, it was unbelievable, because I think what the Tories tried to do at that time under Thatcher in creating Section 28, they created a piece of legislation that was purposefully vague, so because it was purposefully vague and it wasn't concrete people couldn't quite grasp what it was and so it silenced people because they didn't know what they should or shouldn't do.'

So it was ineffective as a law, but highly effective as a deterrent. Sally reflected on how Section 28 shaped her understanding of the work she has been doing:

'The piece of legalisation was very much about limiting the access to information for LGBT young people, and then for LGBT people who had children it was shaming them almost, so again it was

Stop the Clause badge, from Paul Patrick's personal collection

about children and young people and that's what motivated me because that's the area of LGBT communities that I'm interested in.'

> "SECTION 28 WAS ABOUT LIMITING THE ACCESS TO INFORMATION FOR LGBT YOUNG PEOPLE, AND THEN FOR LGBT PEOPLE WHO HAD CHILDREN IT WAS SHAMING THEM ALMOST."
>
> SALLY CARR

Ex-teacher Andrew Dobbin reflected on the personal and work consequences of the law which left him feeling unable to come out: 'I think it was the legacy of Section 28 as well, I didn't know whether I could come out, and I certainly didn't know how to.'

Ali Ronan worked for a local authority and provided a story of how Section 28 led to local conflicts over which projects to support or not, and how some workers' persistence meant that some lesbian and gay youth groups managed to continue despite Section 28:

'I was working in Lancashire at the time and we had a couple of groups for lesbian and gay young people, two or three that I was kind of involved in, but marginally, and at the time our boss in Lancashire wanted to close them down because of Section 28. … It said that you could not talk about homosexuality … as if it was an accepted part of life really … . Obviously we took no notice of it, you couldn't talk about the family. So if you had a gay couple or a lesbian couple you couldn't talk about that as a family … . And of course it was really a paper tiger in that nobody has ever been prosecuted, but it frightened people.'

So what effect did Section 28 have on communities and how did they react? Sue Sanders was in the thick of it and was a part of the foundation of the movement we now know as Stonewall. She provided an insight into how differently gendered political histories played out in the emergence of the movement against Section 28, noting that men had a new-found anger that they needed to channel, and women were grounded in shared networks of grassroots activism through the feminist and the peace movements at the time:

'I know Jill Spraggs in Leicester. I know Paul [Patrick], Julie obviously at the Drill Hall, and we're all beginning to think, "Oh my Goddess, we've got to do something about this." So we set up the Arts Lobby. So Ian McKellen, Michael Cashman, Simon Fanshawe etc meet at the Drill Hall, with Julie Parker, and Julie and I have been very active on the feminist scene. We've been at Greenham. We've done 'Women Against Violence' marches. We've done abortion stuff. I mean, we've been very active radical feminists doing all sorts of stuff, and these boys, know nothing, bless their hearts, except they want to do something about Section 28, which is great.'

But there are fruitful collaborations to be made and knowledge and skills to be shared.

Sue continued:

'So we try and teach them how to be more active, how to do stuff, and what they prove to us is that we know nothing about how Parliament works. We've been so busy doing the grassroots stuff that we haven't educated ourselves about how bills work, who instigates what and so on. It goes to the House of Commons and then it goes to the House of Lords and then? We know nothing about lobbying.'

Sue continued in a way that made her interviewers feel the energy and commitment at the time:

'So they are thinking about that bit. And of course they've got, being in the limelight, fabulous address books with all sorts of interesting people in that we have no access to, so that's all very exciting. So there's this amazing benefit concert at The Palace, at a theatre just on the Embankment, where anybody who is anybody in the arts is at. It raises money and begins to get people to think about the whole issue.

So I'm trying to educate them about schooling. I'm trying to educate them about schools and I'm trying to educate them about inclusivity, because they're constantly going onto programmes and I'm saying, 'You can't all go on. You can't go onto these programmes just as white men. You've got to be inclusive. You've got to have some women there. You've got to have some black people there.' So we're constantly teaching them.

I'm also working with Paul [Patrick] and we're running the London Teachers'

Group. So we're producing pamphlets, we're producing information, we're trying to get the Arts Lobby, who have got much better linkage to the media than we have, [about] how to talk about schools and education, and they can't always hear us.

And I'm going up to the House of Lords and I'm meeting Lord Falkland and other lords and trying to educate them, because it's been passed in the Commons and it's now going up to the Lords. So we're trying to get amendments in that way. And it's massive, you know, enormous demonstrations.'

While Sue and Lena had long histories of activism, it's clear that many people who hadn't considered themselves as political activists were provoked into action. As Lena Milosevic put it:

'The spark was actually Clause 28, and conversations that … Conservative MPs, and Conservative Lords were having, the debates they were having in Parliament and the House of Lords, the language they were using, the kind of fear they were putting about in the community about LGBT people. The misrepresentations, you know, it was all wrong.'

Others, like Brian Jacobs, felt comfortable enough to ignore the clause. Here he remembers how he reacted to a senior teacher who accused him of 'teaching gay sex':

'I hadn't even considered Section 28. I mean … I knew that Section 28 was total nonsense and they couldn't stop teachers promoting homosexuality. And I was in no way going to be muffled by some absurd Section 28 which had long ceased to be of any relevance. But what shocked me about that particular question from a senior teacher was does he think I'm totally insane? He literally thought I was going into a classroom and telling kids how and what gay men do in bed together. I was horrified, needless to say, and I gave him the benefit of my opinion and the question was never raised again. And I actually discussed it later with the Head and I had full support from everybody else and this teacher had to crawl back into his little homophobic hole.'

John Vincent talked about the fear and confusion after 1988, so much so that:

'Lambeth, along with a number of other library authorities got legal advice, which told us that nothing we would do would actually contravene Section 28 because it was a completely useless bit of legislation.'

Former teacher Alan Jackson also told about work going on regardless of Section 28:

'I was a maths teacher so that doesn't give you quite the scope for dealing with things like that, but I was also a sixth form tutor at the time and we did have a pastoral curriculum that included work on sexuality, and that continued. I mean, Section 28 was a con.'

ANTI-SECTION 28 ACTIVISM

Yet despite, and because of, the sense that it was a con many felt the need to protest, like Peter Bradley:

'I went on demos here in Manchester, up and down the land. We campaigned against what was Clause 28 before it was enacted and it became Section 28. So we did that a lot.'

Peter Cookson, who was a former young person of Lesbian and Gay Youth Manchester, and now is a Labour Councillor in Manchester, remembered the strength of feeling in Manchester, and the excitement of the big march:

'We actually were the headquarters for the big anti-Section 28 march that we were expecting, ten or 15,000 people going to come to this and it was a bright, sunny day. [We thought] it'll be a really good number. We got out on the streets, and there were [many more] people on the march; it was absolutely brilliant.'

Rally in Albert Square, Manchester, 20 February 1988, photo from Manchester Archives

According to the website of Gay Birmingham Remembered there were 20,500 people on the Anti-Section 28 demo in Manchester in 1988, making it the biggest LGB demo that had taken place outside the USA. 20,500 is the most quoted figure for the number of demonstrators.

Janet Batsleer captures the paradox, of how Clause 28 united and empowered the LGBT community in activism:

'That year a little group decided they would all get together and take various actions against Clause 28 including going down to London on a big demonstration. We had these placards that said 'Never Going Underground', and they were the same shape as the underground signs that you see outside the underground stations in London.'

'That was great, and the same group got so energised and activated that they ended up with pots of pink paint, and they went up to Queen Victoria's statue, which at that time was in Piccadilly Gardens, and she got drenched, completely drenched in pink paint and had these 'Queen Victoria says Never Going Underground', all around her. So that was really wonderful actually; to see their energy and to see their determination that that attack on young lesbians was not going to go ahead … and really in some way that clause gave rise to a lot more lesbian and gay work. So some people say it stopped people doing things, but I think it made people do things and it was really as a result of that, that a lot more projects and things got off the ground. So you can see it as closing things down but actually it also opened things up. So that's quite an important memory for me.'

REPEAL OF SECTION 28

Whilst the Tories were responsible for Section 28, it was finally repealed in 2003 by the Labour Party. However Tony Fenwick felt that Labour 'dragged its feet' over the issue.

'We all sang along to 'Things Can Only Get Better' in 1997 and hoped this horrible law would be removed forthwith. But there was nothing in the 1997 [Labour Party] manifesto that committed the party to repealing the law. Then they said it was on the back burner because there were so many other things to do. Then again in 2001 it was missing from New Labour's manifesto. The age of consent had been equalised and

Above: Never Going Underground Badge, from Paul Patrick's personal collection

it felt very much like it was… one thing at a time you know?

Finally it was got rid of in the same year they legislated against LGB discrimination in the workplace, but that directive came from Europe; it wasn't home grown. Thinking about how New Labour sought to distance itself from the Party's past, I can't help but feel those at the top in the New Labour Government were trying to fudge the issue. When it came to it, the House of Lords put up a hell of a battle and we worried that it might not go after all. But it still irks that when Labour got in we still had to keep struggling to get Section 28 on the agenda.'

It would be swell to testify that after the repeal of Section 28 our schools became safe spaces for all our communities. This is not the case. Because Local Education Authorities and schools had not embraced their new freedom, in 2005 LGBT History Month was founded by Schools OUT UK. Nigel Tart, maths teacher and former Schools OUT UK Media Secretary:

'You lose a battle and then with Section 28 we knew we weren't going to change schools while that was still in place. There were certain things we could do and we could support each other and encourage people to come out where it was safe and produce resources and advice. But we knew that we had to wait until Section 28 was gone before we could really get going and it was that year when we launched [LGBT] history month [an initiative that seeks to educate out prejudice through LGBT visibility in schools.]'

Armed with an Equalities Act, the Public Sector Equality Duty and a host of legislation and initiatives to awaken schools to the need to embrace equality and diversity, the fight to make schools safe spaces for all our communities still goes on. We cannot imagine a decade and a half without Section 28 and we can only speculate on where we would be had it never happened.

Anti Clause 28 March and Demonstration, London 1988, Rex Features, The Independent

Think of a law we could introduce that would promote LGBT equality. How would you word it?

CHAPTER 5

EdYOUcation

TONY FENWICK

Is the classroom an agency for change or a seat of conformity? Why are so many schools struggling to be safe spaces for their communities? What are the successes and failures, past and present? Can we have a classroom that eliminates prejudice by celebrating equality and diversity in an inclusive environment? How important is LGBT visibility in our schools? What is the relationship between formal and informal education – what can youth work contribute?

From the Prevalence of Homophobia surveys to the Stonewall School Reports and the Teacher Support Network (TSN) teachers survey (and at time of writing the Government is launching yet another survey into the extent of homophobia and transphobia in our schools), we recognise that there is still a long way to go in safely and effectively tackling homophobia and transphobia in the classroom.

The Prevalence of Homophobia surveys are a National Union of Teachers (NUT)/Schools OUT UK based initiative that are carried out in different areas around the country to monitor teachers' views about the extent of homophobia and transphobia in schools and what they think should be done about it. They regularly show that over 90% of teachers see an incident at least once a term and more than half want whole school training to deal with it.

The Stonewall School Reports measure pupils' responses and show that most LGBT pupils are bullied at school.

The Teacher Support Network (TSN) survey in 2007 again measured teachers' responses and showed that homophobia was rife in the classroom.

Despite the opportunities and resources that have been offered to schools including LGBT History Month; International Day against Homophobia, Biphobia and Transphobia (IDAHOBIT); free online lesson plans provided by The Classroom; as well as the disciplinary consequences of The Equality Act Public Sector Equality Duty (PSED) and the latest OFSTED (Office for Standards in Education, Children's Services and Skills) criteria, far too many schools can be viewed as making their LGBT communities invisible.

On the issue of schools' duty to progress equality, Tony Fenwick, Chief Executive Officer (CEO) of LGBT History Month, and a teacher, said:

'So you need to 'promote equal opportunities' and 'foster good relations between the protected characteristics'. Those are not my words, those are the words of the Equality Act, public sector equality duty; they're enshrined in law so every school should be doing that already and every school should be feeding back on what it's doing and how successful it is. Now we know in reality that's not happening so that's something we need to enforce. But also we need to make sure we tell schools that it's mandatory; it's not an option. That's where the Equality Impact Assessments (EIAs) came in. An EIA is where the institution regularly measures the impact its policies – and policy changes – are having on its intended audience. If equality policies are going to work you have to monitor your staff/clients (where possible) to assess their needs and then look at whether what you are doing is having a positive effect. Of course this Government has done away with them – and with a lot of monitoring – because it's too much red tape and the bosses don't like it. But the EIAs gave the Equality Act teeth and they are an essential part of the process. There's not much point in having policies in place if you don't know who they're for or what effect they have…'

Above: LGBT History Month badge 2006, badge illustration by Hebe Phillips

For 15 years a myth was perpetuated that Section 28 stated gays and lesbians couldn't be mentioned in schools, and this is one good reason for the current state of affairs in schools, together with the shocking fact that teachers receive no statutory equality and diversity training.

An additional problem is that schools are often agencies of conformity. Pupils are expected to outdo their peers by running faster and jumping higher, by achieving better results and setting higher goals, but otherwise they sit down/stand up/answer 'Sir' or 'Miss'/line up/wear uniform (according to binary gender rules)/and do as they're told. Or else. While we need rules and regulations, and no one wants to promote anarchy in the classroom, the very nature of schools is that they often end up rewarding conformity and disciplining difference.

The result of this can be institutional heteronormativity and institutional heterosexism and in relation to these institutional homophobia, biphobia and transphobia. We are all different. Schools and staff are not equipped to deal with difference.

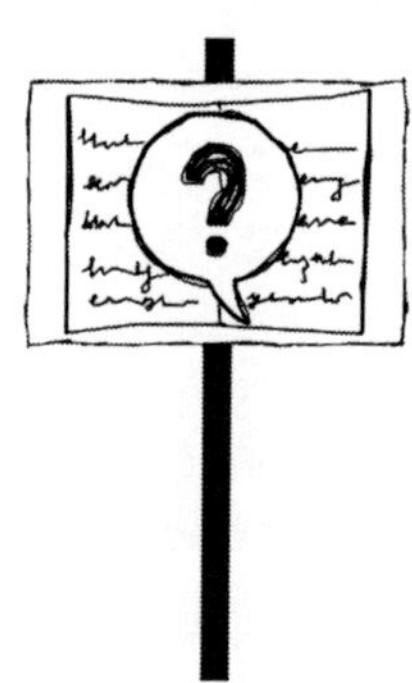

Institutional discrimination: Discriminatory behaviours are 'institutional' when they are part of the structures and procedures of an organisation and impact negatively on people either because of overt prejudice against certain groups, or because of a failure to recognise particular needs of different groups.

Cisgender: A person whose self-identity conforms with the gender that they were assigned at birth.

Heteronormativity: the normalising of heterosexuality, so that other sexualities are made invisible or undermined.

Heterosexism: privileging heterosexuality so the assumption is that everyone is heterosexual in everyday discourse, and alternative sexualities are marginalised or excluded.

homophobia, biphobia and transphobia: hatred and fear of people who are not heterosexual or cisgender.

LGBT YOUTH WORK WORKS

The difficult situation in schools for many LGBT young people has led to the development of an LGBT Youth Movement. Organisations like LGBT Youth North West (LGBTYNW) are essential to young LGBT people who may feel alienated by mainstream education. LGBTYNW's Myrtle Finley describes how it helped her reach her goals when her school had let her down:

'So my involvement in LGYM [Lesbian and Gay Youth Manchester] made such a difference to my life because you know, I left school with not very many GCSEs, I didn't complete my final year, but I was able to get on my path to study through LGBT Youth North West. So I did key skills in things like sexual health or team building or, you know, other things like that, and that helped me. I loved learning and I loved, you know, studying; it was the environment that actually I didn't really thrive in. But coming here and the training that we got as young people, as volunteers, as staff members, has really helped me, so I was able to get onto NVQ courses through my volunteering here, you know, NVQ youth work courses. Now I'm in my final year of my degree. [Since the time of the interview Myrtle has gained a First Class Honours degree in Youth and Community Work.] If I hadn't have been involved in LGBT Youth North West, if I hadn't been involved in LGYM as a young person, I don't know where I would have got that impetus and that support to get to where I am now. So the learning is ongoing and it's massive and it's, you know, community-based as well.'

Although education is a statutory obligation, LGBT youth facilities are not widespread and many areas are less well-served than Manchester and the North West. According to Jenny Anne Bishop, Coordinator of TransForum, Manchester:

'There are other groups I've been to but there is a centre down in Wolverhampton now run by Gender Matters, it's more like this centre [the LGBT Centre in Manchester] but it's specifically for the trans* community. When I lived in the south I didn't easily find LGBT centres. We had a centre down in Cardiff for a while called the

LGBT History Month badge 2007, badge illustration by Hebe Phillips

LGBT History Month badge 2008, badge illustration by Hebe Phillips

LGBT Excellence Centre, and that was quite good, but it was funded by the Welsh government. So they were quite well off but unfortunately they squandered the money and it ran out of funds very suddenly and we were all very sad it disappeared because we had started to build a network of groups across Wales. Fortunately I still know all the people and we've continued with building the network. And the next thing we want to do is to try and build a youth network rather like the UK youth network, because it's sorely needed in Wales, and we've had one or two discussions with Amelia [Lee, youth worker] and others about how we might learn the good practice from the current network, and then link up with the new network in Wales once we get it properly established.'

Myrtle also talked of the growth of trans* awareness among youth groups:

'We get more young people identifying in different ways, you know, in more recent years there's been a lot more young people who have identified as trans* or within the trans* spectrum, and that's really positive. I think that's the change I've seen, quite significantly there's a lot more awareness and understanding of trans* identities and the variety of gender expression and identity. And I think LGBT Youth North West has been really brilliant in bringing that to the fore in terms of local young people and further afield because it's not just about sexual orientation, it's about gender, sometimes they cross over and sometimes they're quite separate. But people do have to come out, people do have to have those similar experiences because of what we're told all the time and because heterosexism exists and the way it manifests is that sometimes there's a confusion between "[Are these] my feelings of attraction for other people or is it actually my identity and my gender?" So it's great that there's spaces like LGBT Youth North West where young people can come and explore that and find where they are and not have to put a name on it, you know, you don't come to the door and people say, "So what are you?" you know, which is a really important thing.'

So LGBT youth groups can give people – particularly but not exclusively trans* people – a possibility to explore their identities in an environment where they can feel safe. Few schools could do that.

"AND OUT OF THAT KIND OF BACKGROUND IS QUITE PROFOUND, YOUR OWN SELF-HATRED."

JEFF EVANS

So what is it like being LGB or T at school and what has changed? Jeff Evans, a former teacher, blamed the heterosexism of the respectable working class for his miserable years:

'I think it's useful to contextualise where I was coming from, I was coming from a working class community, the respectable working class, … the path was very clear as far as sexuality was concerned. You found a nice girl and you settled down, and then you had children. And quite family orientated, and quite a clear machoism as well. And I'd chosen, obviously, consciously chosen that that wasn't for me. And therefore being bullied regularly at school was something that you took with that sense, you know. I had a horrific attendance at school, I think it was down to 60 or 65 percent, I had a day off a week. Why go to school to be bullied? It's as simple as that. And out of that kind of background the homophobia is quite profound, your own self-hatred.'

For Claire Blake, it was the isolation borne of invisibility that hurt the most. She went to school when Section 28 was in force:

'When I was at school there was no information at school, and there was also no information in libraries, and there were no gay characters on television. And I knew how I felt about women, but I didn't know of anybody else that felt the same, so I thought I was on my own. I daren't talk to anybody about it, 'cause I thought this must be something wrong with me basically. And so it was very isolating and very depressing, and I felt that surely something must be up, that something was being concealed, but it was a very difficult position to be in.'

LGBT History Month badge 2009, badge illustration by Hebe Phillips

Liam Mason is a youth worker at LGBTYNW and at the Young People's Advisory Service, Liverpool. He is working towards a Post Graduate Diploma in Youth and Community Work from Manchester Metropolitan University and described how he had to raise questions around gender and sexuality when studying in Autumn 2013:

'But then if I look a bit more recently, so September through to December when I had lectures for my youth and community work course, we didn't have anything which really focused around gender and sexuality or other differences, other than race. We'd have the occasional lecture, which was about sexuality, never covered gender, didn't really cover anything about disability, so for me my main challenge there was, "Right, I need to stand up and say something." At that point it was, "Well, what about sexuality? What about young people who are gay, how do you challenge that? Because actually there were a lot of people who wouldn't understand how to challenge it, wouldn't understand the language behind it to or be able to challenge homophobia. So I think for me, that was a massive challenge, I had to physically say, at pretty much every lecture, "What about this? What about that?"'

For youth worker Sally Carr, addressing LGBT Issues in schools would actually benefit everyone:

'If we work to address homophobia, biphobia, transphobia we actually, and I recognise these other oppressions, we make society better for everyone, not just LGBT people. Because at the root of some of that is the notion of sex, and people get squeamish. When they think about gay sex or lesbian sex, they get squeamish about it. And actually if that was more acceptable and more talked about I think sex and relationships between people on the whole would be better.'

Sally also reflected on informal education channels and how they could be utilised to create a better understanding of LGBT issues and communities:

'I think actually what's happened has been interesting, I think formal education has recognised the value of informal education so I think there's a long way to go but you think about how pupil referral units work, well essentially they are delivering formal education through informal education methods and that to an extent works. I think schools have recognised in some degree a need for youth workers, who can actually work with young people in those very informal ways within that formal institution.'

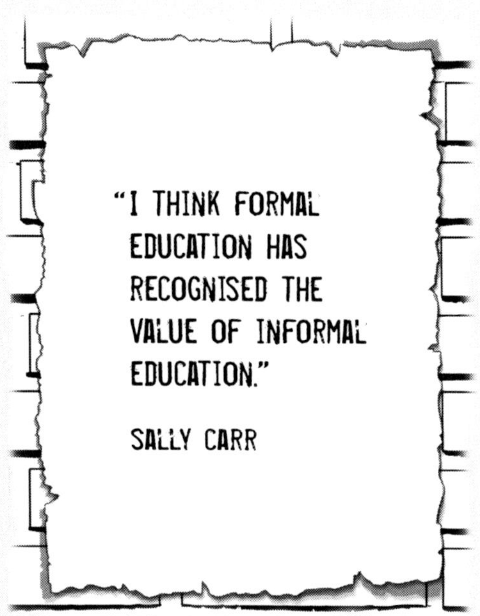

When talking about youth work, Sally praised the work that LGBT Youth North West as an umbrella organisation has done to get peers to promote equality in schools and to create a qualification for this training:

'For our work that we deliver, the schools have seen the value of having youth workers to come in to train young people, for example, to be young ambassadors in Cheshire schools fighting homophobic bullying. I think what youth workers have to do is be able to tell the story of its value in different ways that formal education understands. And some of that is about accredited programmes of work, so we created LGBT Youth College so we do our accredited key skills through Open College, through LGBT Youth College, and school understands that, they understand accreditation. So they can put a value to LGBT youth work other than it being a value in itself; which it is, but in order for them to see the currency of it we've had to put that accreditation in. So I think there's a long way to go but I think those institutions have seen the value and hopefully the value will grow.'

Another area where youth work is essential is in building and repairing relationships with parents. Barbara Spence, the parent of a gay man, described the traditional scenario when LGBT children are invisible in school but discover themselves at university. She went on to say that "parents do need help, some need more help than others."

LGBT parents are starting to make an impact on schools and one thing they are challenging is books that exclusively present families based on heterosexual relationships and in doing so fail to represent a model that LGBT parented children can fully relate to, or that will expose other children to alternative family constructs. No Outsiders challenged this in the early 2000s and The Classroom and Challenging Homophobia in Primary School (CHIPS) are working to combat heterosexism and heteronormativity in the primary sector.

Although, as Jayne Mugglestone testified, parent power itself can be a wonderful thing:

'At my older daughter's school, they've just done a whole LGBT thing. I won't say that was because of me but as soon as she went into Year 7 and it was clear there was loads of homophobic stuff going on, I went in and said, "You know, this is not okay, it's not okay for my daughter." I didn't just stomp in and annoy everybody, I went in, I made friends with all the teachers, I was very kind of clear about this isn't okay, we need to do something.'
'She [Jayne's daughter] just saw everyone going, "Ew, that gay, or this is gay or that's gay" and so she was scared to say that she'd got lesbian mums and a gay dad. But she's very, I wouldn't say honest, I don't mean that other people are dishonest, it's just not in her nature really to hide things. So I said to her, "Well, you know, don't tell people for a bit, just see how you go." But she found that really hard, she wanted to kind of be upfront. And actually everyone that she told was okay with it.'

BEING OUT OR BEING OUTED?

Do teachers need to be 'out' to be good role models? It's not always easy. LGB teachers have only had legal protection in the workplace since 2003 and – although they've had protection since 2000 – transgender teachers are massively underrepresented in the staff rooms of the land and transitioning while in service can be fraught with difficulty.

With no legal protection in the 1970s, 'coming out' could be a career threatening experience for teachers. John Warbuton was barred from working in London schools by the Inner London Education Authority (ILEA) in 1973 for

No Outsiders was a project supporting primary teachers in developing strategies to address lesbian, gay, bisexual and transgender equality in their own schools and classrooms. It ran from 2006 to 2008 and The No Outsiders team, a collaboration of primary education practitioners and university researchers, has taken groundbreaking steps in addressing lesbian, gay, bisexual and trans* equality in primary schools. Books include *Spacegirl Pukes*, *King and King* and *Tango Makes Three*.

The Classroom is a web-based resource for teachers founded by Elly Barnes with lessons that work to usualise and actualise LGBT people in schools and covers all subject areas and Key Stages.
See www.the-classroom.org.uk/

refusing to stay in the closet. This led to the foundation of the Gay Teachers Group, which developed into Schools OUT UK. It began life as a support group for LGB teachers.

Geoff Hardy was a teacher at that time and remembered having to make a decision which would likely result in being outed by the local press in Lewisham:

'I was involved with gay activism and there was a comedian called Larry Grayson who was limp wristed, camp, effeminate and [assumed by others as] weak and he was appearing in Lewisham concert hall. So the local group of people decided to picket it because it was a stereotype in a time when the only thing we were known by was stereotypes. So I went along and the press turned up, the local paper, and it was a decision I had to make at that point in time was, "Do I continue to stand here and hold this placard that says all sorts of people are gay or do I go?" I knew that if I did stay and be photographed it would be in next week's paper which would be seen by the boys I taught and teachers alongside it and their parents, and I also knew John Warburton had been sacked (technically he was not 'sacked', though effectively he couldn't work in any London schools.) I've always operated on the idea that you do what's right and also you don't have a life if you aren't

Supporting Gay Teachers, from Paul Patrick's personal collection

who you are. So I stood there and the following week the photograph appeared and it all started from there.'

So what happened next? Geoff continued:

'I came into the school that day, I remember it so clearly. God, my stomach was churning and, as I walked into the school from playground, you can sense an atmosphere, you know something is going down. It didn't feel friendly or unfriendly, but you just know something is going down. And I went into the school assembly and I do remember the newspaper with that photograph on it going, I hadn't seen it yet, going from lap to lap and this was an educational priority area school, EPA school, so it was a rough all-boys school and I also knew that a fair amount of the staff there were very dyed-in-the-wool conservative with a small 'c' people.

Dyed in the wool: set in one's ways and unlikely to change.

Conservative with a small 'c': traditional in the way one sees the world and resistant to change, but not necessarily a supporter of the Conservative Party.

So how did it go down? Well my first lesson of the day was with third years who these days are, is it, year nine? 14 years old. And I walked towards the classroom door and I looked through the glass and there were all these boys with little banners on rulers that are similar to the banner that I was waving and I thought, "shit!" So I went in the room and said, "For god's sake put those away because you will get me into trouble." So they said, "On one condition, that you share with us and answer questions," and I said, "Yes, on one condition that I don't have to answer the questions that are too personal. I don't want to answer them." So I remember just sitting on the table at the front and I can tell you; Charlton Boys' School was a place where it was a very difficult place to get classroom control. It was not the easiest of schools; they were great kids but they were not the easiest. You really had to entertain them. Total silence. And they are sitting there in their desks in rows and I am talking and they're asking questions, very excellent questions, on how did it feel, when did I know, how does one know, how is it for you, do you have a boyfriend, all sorts of stuff. And by the end of – I think it was about 70 minutes to 80 minutes (they were long, long lessons) – there was a horseshoe of them. They had moved forward and they were sitting in front of me and a couple of them were nearly in tears. There wasn't a single homophobic comment.'

This remarkably uplifting story reminds us that when we give young people knowledge we empower them and they respect us for that.

Lena Milosevic was a Leicester teacher who came out at a National Union of Teachers (NUT) conference during the discussion of a motion opposing Section 28. The Union's executive was not especially supportive. Leicester Authority described her decision as unwise and questioned whether she should be allowed to continue to teach (although they did concede they had no plans to sack her). Here she describes her return to her school when the Conference was over:

'And this was all young people, they were like 11 to 18 year olds, it was a secondary school. And I can remember real nerves and I was teaching English and being in one classroom. You're at the front as the teacher and the kids are all piling in. And my heart was racing. And one lad piped up, "Ah Miss is a lessie" and immediately this boy from the back row said, "Oh shut up, Miss is all right," just kind of "shut up, Miss is all right." And that really was the end of it.'

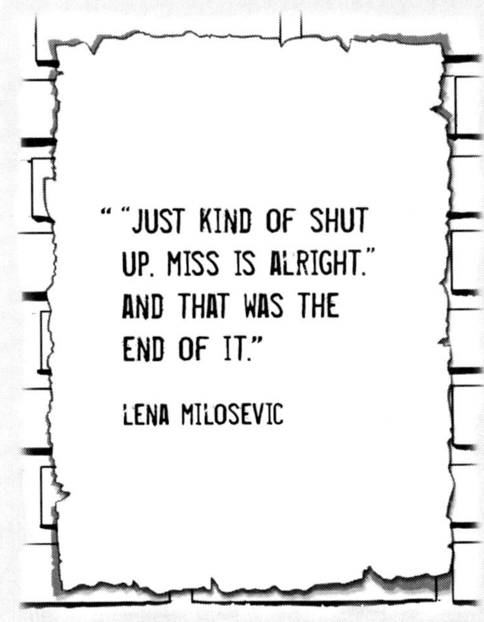

LGBT history month 2010 lesbian gay bisexual trans

Tony Fenwick talked about why he thought it was important for teachers to come out, both for pupils and for teachers themselves:

'I was at a conference where I remember one teacher standing up saying, "What's all this fuss about coming out at school? It's nobody's business what your sexual orientation is. Why is there all this pressure to come out?" And I think, well it reminds me of when I was in the '70s at school. I was at secondary school in the 1970s and we had a teacher who was married and his wife was a teacher. I don't know about her but he was definitely gay and he was living the life of a heterosexual in a heterosexual way and doing all the things that heterosexuals do. We knew he was gay. You just knew, gaydar, call it what you will, you just knew. That told me as a teenager who was growing up and realising my sexual orientation - 'cause I preferred boys to girls and there was no question about that. That told me as a young teenager in that situation that if I was gay I had to keep my head under the parapet, the safest thing was to keep in the closet, shut it all down and not let anybody know. And that's why it's important for teachers to come out, because the kids know, they can tell and if you're living a lie; they know it; they can see it. Also it's bad for your health if you're living a lie. I remember when I joined Schools Out [now Schools OUT UK] a lesbian teacher told me that she had a big challenge because she had a long term illness in a school where she'd worked for a long time and her colleagues wanted to come and visit her, bring her flowers, chocolates etc. and say hello and find out how she was getting on when she was recovering. She felt she couldn't let them in

"WE KNEW HE WAS GAY. YOU JUST KNEW, GAYDAR, CALL IT WHAT YOU WILL, YOU JUST KNEW."

TONY FENWICK

'cause she had a female partner living in the house with her and because she'd been in the closet for so long she didn't feel safe to come out. And of course people perceive that as her being offhand perhaps or cold. And you know, it affects the way you live and it affects your self-confidence and it's very, very important that people are able to come up. That's also a benchmark of the school because if people don't feel safe to come out then there's something wrong with the institution, there's some kind of institutional homophobia going on in there, which needs to be worked on.'

Peter Tatchell provided a rather more optimistic story of the difference that transformed cultures in schools can make:

'A school in North London I went to some time ago had a real big problem with homophobic and transphobic bullying. There were no pupils who were openly gay. But some pupils were 'suspected' of being LGBT and teased as a result, and the school authorities really were trying to tackle it but didn't make much progress. So on the initiative of both staff and pupils they set up an LGBT straight alliance. Now interestingly this was led by two young Muslim girls, they led the way in setting up the Gay Straight Alliance and they got a lot of flack. But they persevered and in a year or so four pupils came out and gradually the atmosphere in the school began to change.
You know, it went from a school where homophobic and transphobic bullying was rife and was

Above left: LGBT History Month badge 2010

Above right: LGBT History Month badge 2011

Bottom right: LGBT History Month badge 2012,
badge illustrations by Hebe Phillips

virtually unchallenged to a situation where peer pressure began to make it unacceptable, so much so that, [as] I said, four LGBT pupils were able to come out.'

A Gay-Straight Alliance is a peer led initiative in schools where LGBT people and their non-LGBT allies join together to support making their schools safe for LGBT people, through challenging heterosexism, and homophobia. They usually meet regularly and organise promotional events. They have been in existence for some years in the USA and Canada but they are just starting to gain ground in the UK.

Another initiative transforming schools is the Public Sector Equality Duty (PSED). The PSED expects, amongst other things, that schools 'foster good relations [between people who share a protected characteristic and those who do not.] This means Heads and teachers going out into the community and meeting its leaders and representatives to achieve community cohesion – and this process has only just begun, but is a crucial step in linking what happens within schools, with what is happening in the wider world. Sue Sanders used the issue of hate crime legislation to reveal the seriousness of homophobic bullying in schools. The paradox here is that schools effectively protect the protagonists within their walls when the acts they commit would lead to criminal convictions and cautions were they to take place outside school premises: "So what they call bullying, if it happened on the

LGBT History Month badge 2013, badge illustration by Hebe Phillips

street would be a crime, and they don't see that or they don't take it on board, many schools, not all but some."

LGBT History Month badge 2014 badge illustration by Hebe Phillips

Peter concurred:

'You know, when we think about homophobic and transphobic bullying we've got to remember that if it was happening outside the school environment in the street, a factory or an office it would be deemed a hate crime and the perpetrator would probably be prosecuted. Now I'm not saying pupils who, you know, abuse other LGBT pupils should be prosecuted, but certainly action needs to be taken, certainly that needs to be challenged, they need some sort of disciplinary steps taken. But most importantly they need education about the issues, they need to be informed, they need to be engaged, they need to be challenged, they need to be forced to understand the adverse impact of what they are doing and saying.'

Both agree that teaching that discrimination and prejudice are wrong is – or should be – a part of the curriculum. Sue again:

'Schools OUT UK has been passionate for years saying anti-bullying work, when it is after the effect, is pretty ineffectual. What we should be doing is, which is one of our straplines, is educate out prejudice. So the work should be in school, in the curriculum, enabling people to dissect and … [ask] "What is discrimination?" "What is bullying?" "What feeds that?" and actually educate out prejudice, all forms, not just homophobia and transphobia but racism, sexism, disablism, gothicism, you know, all that stuff.'

Peter concluded:

'I think that education is really the key to overcoming homophobic and transphobic bullying. Not so much the threat of disciplinary action, although there's a place for that and it is necessary, but really to change hearts and

LGBT History Month badge 2015, badge illustration by Hebe Phillips

minds, that's the key way forward To provide a safe, welcoming environment for LGBT staff and pupils.'

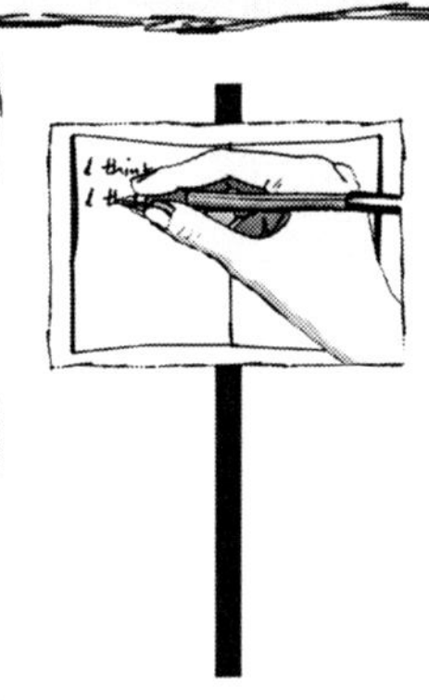

What did/does your school or college do to make it an LGBT inclusive space? What would you like to see them do? Could you support this in any way?

CHAPTER 6

TRIALS AND TRIBULATIONS

THE DIFFICULTIES AND COLLABORATIONS WITHIN THE LGBT COMMUNITY

LIAM MASON

''Cause you had the gay men who didn't like women, you'd have racist gays, you'd have the women that didn't like transsexuals and transvestites in those days.'
Peter Cookson

This is our starting point, minorities fighting minorities. Progress in collaboration has been slow and fraught with tensions. But progress has happened through education and the realisation that we are fighting the same fight. It is also through the increased visibility of the 'L', the 'G', the 'B' and the 'T'. This provides the foundations for future activism within the LGBT community.

While there is/was both conflict and cohesion amongst the L, G, B and T communities, it is important also to consider the individual identities which make up the LGBT community. These entities are not separate, but integral and inseparable. Members of the LGBT community represent different classes, cultures, histories, abilities and privileges. These differences have enabled the community to question, learn, educate and strengthen the political movement. The journey to where we are today has been both joyful and painful, including times of disagreement, misunderstanding and lack of representation. It is vital to remember those who have fought for their own individual

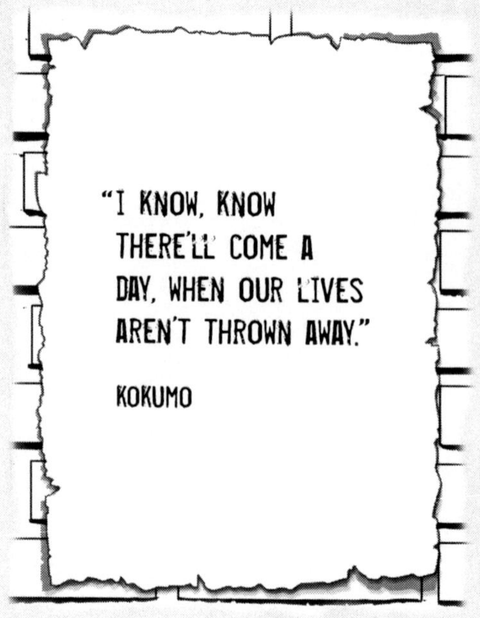

rights, rights of the LGBT community, the disabled community, women's movements, class rights, and for those from many different races, ethnicities and cultures who have come together to support each other and fight for their rights.

'There Will Come a Day' expresses the hope of a better life for trans* women of colour, and Kokumo, trans* singer, mourns those who have died from transphobic violence.

Lesbian: A woman who is attracted to women.

Gay: A man who is attracted men.

Bisexual: A person who is attracted to both men and women.

Trans*: an inclusive umbrella term for people who have a gender identity (internal sense of self) that is different to the gender they were assigned at birth.

Intersectionality: is a concept used to describe the ways in which oppressions (racism, sexism, homo/bi/transphobia, ableism, xenophobia, classism etc.) are interconnected and cannot be examined separately from one another.

In 1967 homosexuality was decriminalised for gay men over the age of 21. (Lesbianism had never been criminalised.) Men at this time were still the privileged gender, and sexism was rife. So what if you met a trans* person, or a person from the just as invisible bisexual community?

Janet Batsleer, Lecturer in Youth and Community Work at Manchester Metropolitan University, had this to say:

'Were there conflicts in the community? Lots and lots and lots and lots and lots and lots and lots. So probably there would be conflicts around radical lesbians versus gay men and then radical lesbians versus S & M dykes.'

This highlights but a few of the conflicts that faced the progression of the LGBT community. Why were there so many problems in coming together for a common cause? Brazilian educator and philosopher Paulo Freire suggests, in his 1972 book *Pedagogy of the Oppressed,* that an already oppressed group will ultimately find another smaller minority to oppress. The themes of power and influence will be explored in this chapter as they have been prominent in the reflections of members of the LGBT community.

Nigel Leach, a youth worker, says:

'People are a bit territorial about their influence and their bit of power, and don't want to give it up particularly when they're asked to share resources and things like that.'

The setting up of lesbian and gay groups, even though resources were scarce, had a massive impact on the LGBT community. The groups were safe spaces where young people could come and share experiences without judgement. From the criminalisation of homosexuality through to today, LGBT people often have internalised homophobia and self-hatred. This is through the societal representation of the LGBT community; there is an assumption that everyone is heterosexual. Internalised homophobia has a negative impact on mental and sometimes physical wellbeing. Youth workers running the first lesbian and gay groups were often working through their own acceptance of being homosexual. This could often lead to burn-out from the lack of personal support, and the need to take on a lot of responsibility for the well-being of young people without the financial backing or resources.

GAY MEN VERSUS LESBIAN WOMEN

Nigel remembers, speaking generally about society in the 1970s and '80s, that 'people tended to focus on the men as well didn't they, and they knew certainly it was more about gay males than it was lesbian women.' This focus on gay men perpetuated the separation between the lesbian and gay communities and compounded the misogynistic views of many men and the trans* misogynistic view of some feminists.

Tim Lucas, an LGBT activist, recalls:

'A lot of gay men were misogynists, there's no question about that. There was just a kind of unspoken mutual agreement to live separately, somehow. I mean in terms of the support line, you know, there was a gay switchboard, there was a separate lesbian line.'

Misogynist: A person who hates women.

Trans* misogyny: Discrimination against trans* people, for example, stating that a trans* woman will never be a 'real' woman and will not be accepted as a woman.

As does Peter Cookson:

'You had quite a lot of radical feminists, and their view was that the trans* community were perpetuating the traditional image of women. So that was a conflict as well, so you had all this going on when we're all trying to fight the same fight, so it was chaos.'

Reflecting back on the idea of oppressing the oppressed, could the energy used on fighting against each other and fighting an individual fight been used in a better way? Arguably, if we did not have this turbulent time would it have been clear that the gay and lesbian community were fighting for the same thing? Would society have been ready to open their minds to a sexuality that had only just been decriminalised? Progress in society will only go as fast as those outside of the minority will allow it. Laws can change. Education and 'usualisation' can happen. Young people can come together in youth groups. But it takes time and greater visibility of the community to create a foundation of change.

Usualising: to make usual/everyday/ubiquitous. It is the non-comment, the non-judgement, the non-reaction. It is the inclusion through reference, not instruction. It is the tacit approval of acceptability, and it must be used frequently for that acceptance to be embedded in the learner.

Usualising LGBT lives means that learners are made aware of the diversity of LGBT people, that they are found in every culture, near and far, and that they share many characteristics with people who are heterosexual. It is also about acknowledging the differences between LGBT individuals themselves, that they do not all conform to the same behaviours/appearance. In this way usualising tackles prejudice. Usualising can be used to make visible any minority group.

Actualising: presenting the subject in some fuller aspect. It should include the positives and negatives as well. We are not making value judgements, nor are we encouraging bias in favour of LGBT life by ONLY representing positive images of LGBT people.

Definitions taken from www.the-classroom.org.uk

THINK ABOUT WHO YOU ARE.
DO YOU FACE PREJUDICE FROM SOCIETY?
WHAT WOULD YOU DO TO CREATE A CHANGE?

THE COMING TOGETHER OF THE L THE G AND THE B

In the late 1980s LGB became a more commonly used term. Before this, the B for bisexual was very much invisible. This was the starting point for the heterosexual and homosexual communities to understand and recognise that there are a multitude of different sexualities and everyone is different. When youth groups became LGB groups it allowed young people the safe space to explore their sexuality and to share experiences. The barriers between the polar opposites of sexuality that had existed for years were beginning to be broken down.

Unfortunately, one could argue we are still a long way off the full acceptance of those who identify as bisexual, or in fact people who have a sexuality that does not conform to heterosexual and homosexual.

The media plays a role in increasing bisexual invisibility and erasure. Maeve Bishop highlights Netflix's *Orange is the New Black,* a show in which the main character is bisexual. She is represented as heterosexual at the start of the show as she is with her male fiancée. It is presumed that she has "become" lesbian again as the show focuses on her imprisonment alongside her ex-girlfriend. This highlights the way in which the media is re-enforcing the expectations that you are either heterosexual or homosexual and that is all.

CONSIDER HOW THIS SHOW COULD HAVE BEEN WRITTEN TO BETTER REPRESENT BISEXUAL PEOPLE?

It is important to remember that we are able to define ourselves. Although, this can at times be challenging, as Maeve Bishop tells us:

'I am not straight but I'm not a lesbian, I wouldn't really define as bisexual and people are like, "Oh, so you're this?" It's like, "No, stop trying to put me in the box, like I'm not defined by my partner, I'm defined by me."'

Maeve point is valid and reflects a wider problem. Generally speaking, society likes to put people in boxes and place labels on them. By doing this

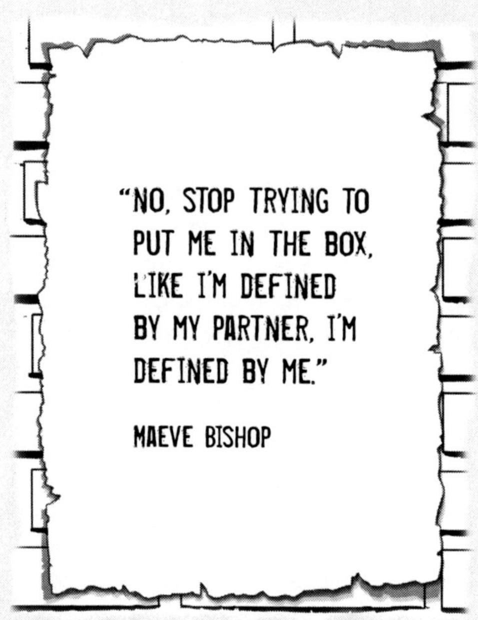

it is easier to make sense of the world. Unfortunately everyone is an individual and therefore not everyone fits neatly into the prescribed boxes. However, it is also important to note that although we define ourselves, for some, a partner can help us to understand ourselves and our identity.

THE T, TENTATIVELY ADDED

Barbara Spence, was a member of the Manchester Parents' Group:

'We decided that we knew about the L, we knew about the G, we knew about the B. We didn't know about the T, so we went along to TransForum and spent a very informative afternoon with them finding out all about it.'

This acceptance of trans* by the Parents' Group that Barbara formed was rare. Initially trans* was often seen as something 'strange' or 'weird'. It has taken a long time for trans* to be fully embraced in the LGBT community and only recently has it become a more focal point in LGBT youth work.

People are brought up in a world of gender stereotypes which they must conform to. There is a lack of knowledge in all communities about the issues of gender identity. It has been in the last five years or so that we have seen the emergence of trans* youth groups, as Ali Ronan, Lecturer in Community and Youth Work, recalls:

'[It used to be] the lesbian and gay group and then it became the lesbian, gay and bisexual group so people had to question themselves about that, and then now it's got the T on as well and I think well how fantastic because this is another space where people feel that they can be themselves.'

Pronoun: a pronoun is the word used to describe you when your name is not used. In English, and in many languages, pronouns are gendered. There are feminine pronouns: she/her/hers; masculine pronouns: he/him/his and gender neutral pronouns: they/them/theirs. Some people also prefer not to have a pronoun used for them but would rather their name was used.

PRONOUNS

Trans* groups and trans* aware LGBT groups are sometimes the only place where trans* people can be out as their preferred gender, using their preferred name and pronoun.

HOW OFTEN DO YOU HEAR 'HIM' AND 'HER' BEING USED WHEN OTHERS ARE TALKING ABOUT YOU?

HAVE YOU EVER CONSIDERED ITS USE AND HOW IT MAKES YOU FEEL?

It can be tricky to change the pronoun used to describe people but it is one of the most important things that people can do if they know anyone who comes out as trans* and they ask you to use a different pronoun. The difficulty comes when there is a refusal to accept and use a new pronoun for someone you know. This could be through not understanding what a pronoun is or not understanding the importance of a pronoun in validating an identity.

There is now more awareness of gender diversity. Young people are starting to receive workshops on gender identity in schools. There is far more acceptance of a trans* person who is transitioning so long as they fit into the 'neat' boxes of man and woman, however, there is still a lot less collective understanding of non-binary gender identities. As Tony Fenwick describes:

'There's also an issue of people who don't see themselves either inside the gender binary or just going to say, "Well I might transition, I don't know if I want to, maybe I don't want to. Maybe I'm living as a man but I've not had deed poll," things like that.'

Non-binary gender identity: having a gender identity that refuses the binary of male and female. People with a non-binary gender identity may be neither male nor female, or may identify as both male and female, or as some these identities some of the time, or as something else entirely, not captured by the terms male or female. It can also mean the refusal of masculine and feminine gender roles.

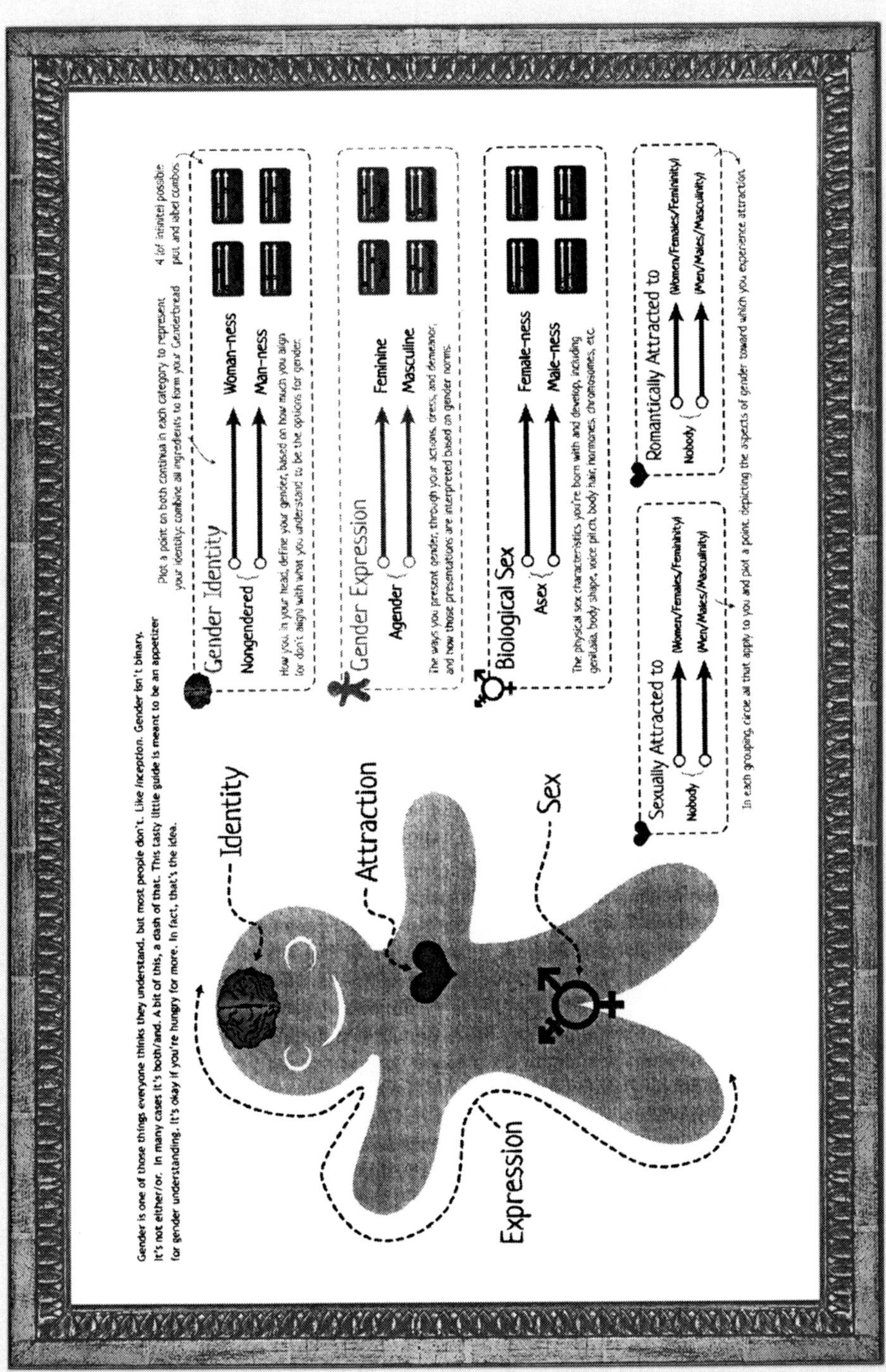

The Genderbread Person version 3.3 www.itspronouncedmetrosexual.com

Gender Identity	This is the internal sense of gendered self; this might be male, or female, or something else. Gender identity is usually attributed at birth on the basis of biological sex. But for many trans* people this does not correspond with how they feel as they grow up.
Gender Expression	This is how gender is on the outside, such as your clothes, your mannerisms and speech. This could be masculine, feminine or androgynous (neither masculine or feminine OR the mixture of both), or not always constant, and changing.
Biological sex	Gender identity is often assigned at birth on the basis of assumptions about biological sex, involving physiological characteristics, and sometimes hormone levels, chromosomes and primary and secondary sex characteristics. Often there is an assumption that there is a correlation between what is understood as 'biological sex' and gender identity, so that crudely someone born with a penis is assigned a male identity; and someone one born with a vagina is female. The dominance of gender binaries means that people born with more indeterminate 'biologies' are usually assigned to the categories of either male or female in any case.
Sexually attracted to	The people you are attracted to and want to be sexually intimate with. Sometimes this is combined with emotional or romantic attachment, but not always.
Romantically attracted to	The people that you want to form a deep emotional caring relationship with. Sexual intimacy may or may not not be the main attraction.

Read the comments on the website and reflect further on:

How does the genderbread exercise help you think about gender?

Read the comments on the website and reflect further on:

Does the genderbread diagram have any limitations for you?

HOW WOULD YOU CHANGE THE GENDERBREAD EXERCISE?

The Genderbread activity on pages 99-102 is a reflective task for everyone to consider their own gender, and through this how they might understand other people's varied gender and sexual identities. Below in an explanation of what each section means.

Think about the descriptions on page100 while you work through the genderbread exercise.

Gender is very complicated and there are still gaps on this diagram. Some people will be able to plot themselves on this diagram, others may not. Gender identity is so unique and varied, that it can be hard to reflect everyone's personal identities. This tool however is useful in showing that gender, sexuality and expression are different. There is a lot of discussion on the genderbread exercise website about how useful the genderbread is, and what changes could be made to it.

FROM L 'VS' G TO LGBT - WHERE ARE WE TODAY

This chapter started by exploring the conflicts between the lesbian and gay communities, then the increase of bisexual and trans* visibility, though in reality the history is messy. The way forward is just a messy as there are new issues and conflicts arising, such as same-sex marriage. Trans* people are still discriminated against when it comes to marriage as (if they are already married when they decide to come out as trans*) they have to have their spouses consent to obtain a Gender Recognition Certificate. Each community within the LGBT community has commonalities but also differences and it is important to remember this when working together.

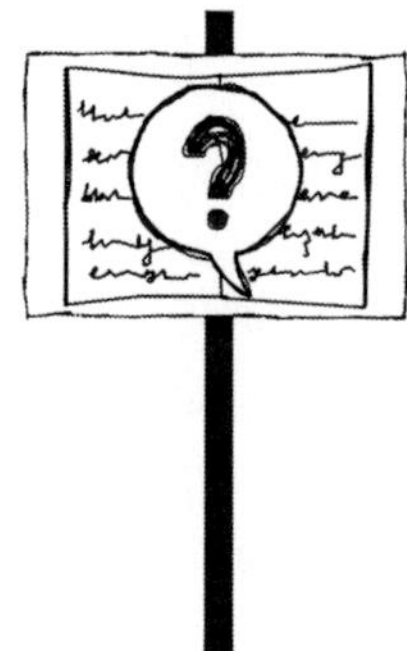

Gender Recognition Certificate (GRC): A certificate that is issued to a trans* person to act as evidence that they are trans*. This certificate can only be obtained after they have lived in their acquired gender role for a minimum of two years. This enables them to have their birth certificate re-issued in their chosen name and gender.

Pansexual: attraction to all genders.

Asexual: the absence of sexual attraction, this does not mean an asexual person cannot form romantic relationships, or sometimes have sexual relationships.

Polyamory: having multiple sexual or romantic relationships that are communicated to each partner and consented to.

Queer: This term has both positive and negative connotations. The positive connotations are that the term is being reclaimed and often used to bring together gender identities and sexual orientations that are outside what society expects. The term queer, however, is still often used as a homophobic term. It has been used in the past to mean odd or weird.

Where we are today:

Several interviewees were asked what changes, if any, they would make to the LGBT community. Here are the responses, respectively, from Amelia Lee, Tony Fenwick, Liam Mason and Ali Ronan:

'That we could all trust each other because too often we fight against each other, even though what we should be fighting against is heterosexism, homophobia, biphobia, transphobia and sexism, which are all bound up in the same thing, right? So if we all group together and trusted each other and were trustworthy then we'd be a much stronger united force.'

'You need to respect and promote equality of opportunity and promote equalities and good relations between the protected characteristics. It's okay to be different, difference is good. I'm different to you or I'm different from you, we've got to celebrate the difference.'

'I became the first full-time trans* worker, which is quite ground-breaking because nowhere else in the country has had this so far, and especially as it is being funded by CAMHS, which is Child & Adolescent Mental Health Services. It's showing that a regional area of the NHS is actually saying, "This is a problem and we want to help solve it," which is amazing.'

'The movement has been about people recognising the need, you know, first it was about women-only space, then it's about lesbian-only space, then it's about lesbian and gay space, then it's about lesbian and gay, bisexual space and then it's about…, so each group seems to me to have built on the fight of the other really.'

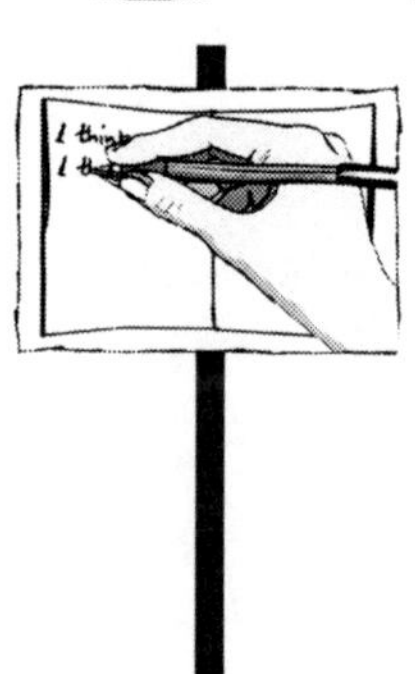

Can you list five things that could be difficult for a trans* person, and consider how you could change each of them.

Problem	**How it could be changed**
Eg: Using gendered toilets	Make gender neutral toilets that are only cubicles
1.	
2.	
3.	
4.	
5.	

CHAPTER 7

JOURNEY TO THE GAY CENTRE OF THE EARTH

HANNAH BERRY

'To sum it up? It's a home, it's a family, and it's a hopeful place I think.'
Myrtle Finley

The official name of the yellow brick building on Sidney Street in Manchester, opposite the soon-to-be-demolished Manchester Metropolitan University (MMU) Students Union, is the Joyce Layland LGBT Centre. However, post still arrives there marked 'The Gay Centre', recalling other, earlier phases in the life of this significant local resource.

How did it all begin? In 1964, a group of men and women in Manchester started the North Western Homosexual Law Reform Committee (NWHLRC), a branch of the Homosexual Law Reform Society (HLRS). When the Sexual Offences Act was passed in 1967, HLRS wound itself up, but the NWHLRC felt there was still rather a lot to do. They rebranded as the Committee (later Campaign) for Homosexual Equality (CHE), which quickly became a national organisation, with local groups all around the country. In 1971 CHE set up a separate counselling and befriending organisation called Friend, and Manchester soon had a local Friend group as well.

The 1967 Sexual Offences Act provided for a limited decriminalisation of homosexual acts between men where these 1) were consensual, 2) took place in private (this excluded hotel rooms and stipulated that no one else could be present in the house, even in another room) and 3) involved people aged 21 or over i.e. 5 years older than anyone else had to be. Sex between two women had never been criminalised.

GAY CENTRE: WATERLOO PLACE - 1970S

CHE also nurtured a Homophile Society at the University of Manchester around this time. The links between activists and students led to the Students' Union offering Friend use of a property it owned on Oxford Road, as Terry Waller explains:

'Initially [there were] the phone lines, the Friend counselling phone line, which obviously the CHE had started and was in Waterloo Place, 178 Oxford Road [Manchester], with the Friend group upstairs answering the phone and offering to meet people to be a friend and counsellor. I wasn't involved in that, but then we started Manchester Gay Switchboard in another rent-free room in the same building and did the Switchboard, which started on 2nd January 1975. Manchester Gay Alliance group, which consisted of the Manchester Lesbians Group, the TV/TS [Transvestites / Transsexuals] group, the University gay soc [the Homophile Society], the CHE group – about five groups – got together, and when Grassroots bookshop left the basement of 178 Oxford Road, said, "We can have the basement, let's all get together," and that was the first Gay Centre. Then John Cotterill applied for the grant in 1978, which paid for a worker who turned out to be Bob Crossman. And then after Bob, Ros, and then after Ros, Paul Fairweather, and then after that in 1985, me. So to say how did I come across the centre … the true answer would by being one of the many dozens of people who helped to start it.'

Top and middle images: Manchester Gay Centre Annual Reports

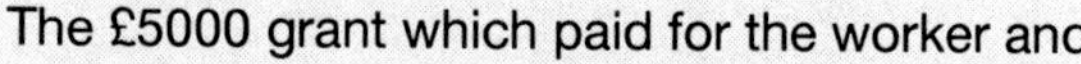

The £5000 grant which paid for the worker and

drew the groups together under the Gay Centre banner, was from Manchester City Council (from their share of the national 'Urban Fund', according to reports). Over the next three years Friend also started a youth group, which ran on Thursday evenings and Saturday afternoons, and a gay men's coming out group called Icebreakers. In 1978 TV/TS began its own telephone helpline there. Barbara, the main volunteer there, looked after it for decades. Even after moving to Edinburgh in her seventies, she continued to drive to Manchester and back every Wednesday to staff the helpline.

While 'gay' in theory meant same sex attraction among either sex, the term was usually used to refer to a gay man or gay men. The youth group was ostensibly mixed, but archives suggest that most centre users and volunteers were men at that time. 21 year old Switchboard volunteer Terry Waller attended the youth group with a friend but he can't quite recollect if they ran it, or if it just ran itself! In 1979 a group of women from Switchboard and Friend formed Lesbian Link, which began its own helpline (and its own discos – a common 1970s combination!) with a further grant from the Council.

GAY CENTRE: BLOOM STREET - 1980S

The Gay Centre relocated to 61A Bloom Street in 1981. It was another "dingy basement", but more spacious. It housed Lesbian Link, Switchboard, Friend, a number of meeting rooms and a late night café bar called SNAX. Mancunian Gay magazine (later Gay Life magazine) was launched from the centre, as was Lesbian Express, which ran for three issues.

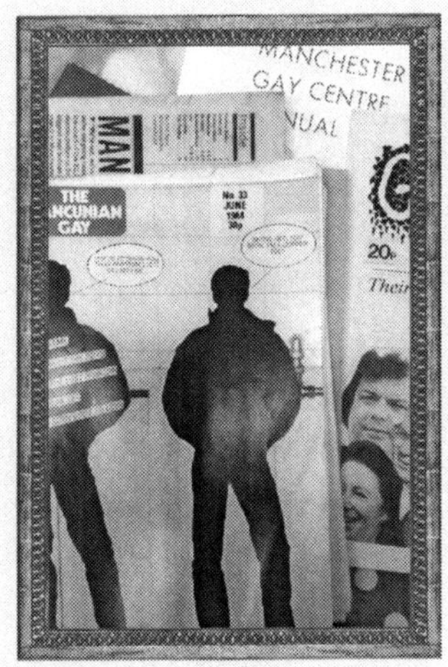

The Mancunian Gay
Thanks to Terry Waller, Nigel Leech, John Cotterill, Paul Fairweather

Peter Cookson remembers his youth club days at Bloom Street:

'We had games, had a television, so sometimes we'd get a video in and watch a film in the afternoon. We'd have political discussion quite a lot because of the time we were in. We'd have entertainment, which one day I provided 'cause I used to be a stand up poet back in those days.

And we had another lad who was a folk singer, so he did a spot. We put on little sketches, plays and things, comedy… we had games, we had table tennis and we had pool, oh snooker it was, a six foot snooker table.'

In 1986 Nigel Leach became the centre's first sessional youth worker, employed by the Community Education Service. In fact, it may have been the first LGBT youth work post in the country. Nigel had started as a volunteer, and continued to volunteer outside of his paid hours, but the values instilled by professional youth work training, those of democracy, empowerment and inclusivity, produced some tensions, as he explains:

'Before there were sessional volunteers, some of the volunteers were from the helpline, some were parents, and some were concerned individuals, people already involved. There was a period where there was quite a lot of resistance from some of the earlier volunteers, who'd been doing a good job to be fair to them.'

The concern of the new sessional workers like Nigel was to avoid 'coming in like a new broom' but to nevertheless try and change the culture a bit, to make it less paternalistic and give the young people more autonomy:

'If parents had their own issues, for example, they were better served by setting up a parents' group where they could think about their own issues and not offload that onto younger people.'

The 1980s were a time of upheaval. HIV became a major focus of volunteering and activism and people from the Gay Centre were at the forefront. A group from the Gay Centre set up Manchester AIDS line in 1985 (which later gave rise to the George House Trust (GHT) and Body Positive). One interviewee recalls a 'jumble sale' on Canal Street in August 1984, the seed from which grew Manchester's annual Pride extravaganza. Nigel got his wish: Manchester Parents' Group was set up by four of the mums – Joyce Layland, Kath Hall, Bernadette Cookson and Joan Cotterill. Joyce and Kath became powerful voices in the movement against Section 28 when that erupted in 1988. In March that year 20,500 people took to the streets in the biggest LGBT rally Manchester has ever seen, marking the start of the national campaign against Section 28, which was headquartered at the Gay Centre on Bloom Street.

Activist Terry Waller remembers:

'Gay Pride' - In 1984 activists and volunteers organised a few stalls outside the Rembrandt Hotel, to raise money for HIV and AIDS causes; another little market "with a tombola" was held in Sackville Park in 1985. It was only in 1991 that the event expanded to include a full programme of activities over the August Bank Holiday. Initially designated 'Carnival of Fun' by the Village Charity, the event became known as Gayfest, Mardi Gras and finally Manchester Pride.

'My first gay paid job was the liaison officer at Bloom Street in 1985 to 1989. This whole kind of media thing and the HIV witch hunt frenzy of that era was now in full swing, where all the tabloids were full, for a period, full of stories, which went something like "Infected HIV person uses swimming pool, schools stop visits to swimming pools"... A kind of climate where we had Manchester's Chief Constable James Anderton – who talked to God, who publicly said God spoke to him – saying that people with HIV were "Swirling about in a cess pool of their own making". That's your Chief Constable.'

Manchester's local authority was opposed to the direction the country was moving in, economically and socially, under the government of Margaret Thatcher (who in 1986 defended Anderton and brushed off calls for a public inquiry).They felt a responsibility to provide for the lesbian and gay people who were increasingly adopting the city as their home. The city had 12 LGBT councillors in 2014, but in 1986 it was heterosexual councillors with a strong commitment to social justice and equality who pushed the policies through.

Paul Fairweather stated that:

'I think at the time the City Council was doing a whole range of very radical policies around equal opportunities, around police monitoring, around neighbourhood services… It was one of a number of councils, Ken Livingstone was head of the Greater London Council, there were a few Labour councils up in our country doing a lot of very radical policies around social policy, and Manchester was probably in some ways the most radical, certainly on lesbian and gay issues. We had one of the first councils to have specific lesbian and gay workers.

In 1985 Graham Stringer became leader of the Council, and a group of us who'd been involved since the early 1980s, involved in the Labour Party in Manchester in campaigning for lesbian and gay rights, we held a series of public meetings... there was actually a meeting for women and a meeting for men. And we set up a formal subcommittee of the council, a Gay Men's Subcommittee, and a separate Lesbian Subcommittee, also the Equal Opportunities Committee, and the Council set up an Equalities Unit and employed two lesbian officers and two gay male officers. I was one of those two gay male officers. But before then, from 1980, I'd been working at the Gay Centre in Bloom Street, so I worked there for five years and then became one of the gay men's officers. And one of the key things on our work programme was actually having a much better gay centre, 'cause Bloom Street was in a quite small place, it was in a dingy basement, so we wanted somewhere that was bigger. We wanted the Council to fund and build a gay centre, so we'd have more security in the long term.'

THE GAY CENTRE MUST BE BUILT!

As the Bloom Street liaison officer, it fell to Terry Waller to campaign for a purpose-built centre. His friend John Shires, a Labour Party activist, advised him to make sure that wherever councillors went – ward meetings, Executive meetings etc. – they heard the message: 'FUND SIDNEY STREET!'

In fact, Sidney Street was not the first location considered. The City Council initially offered £12,000 for a derelict Canal Street site where the Manto bar is now, but it was rejected by the landowners. Sidney Street was the eventual choice because the lot was empty (it once housed a synagogue, then a hotel…) and it already belonged to the Council. This put an end to arguments about whether it was better to stay within the 'safe zone' of what was rapidly developing into the Gay Village, or go somewhere more 'neutral', as Nigel Leach recalls:

'Initially I think people saw this as a bit far away [from the gay bars]... On the other hand an important aspect, certainly for women's groups, also to some extent with the young people, is the whole concept of safety – would it be better to have it slightly away from the commercial area and actually have a place where they perhaps wouldn't be seen coming into the building.'

The empty Sidney Street site, circa 1985

Paul Fairweather remembers the move to build a gay centre being controversial:

'The Manchester Evening News was very hostile, they did an editorial complaining the City Council was trying to turn Manchester into San Francisco... it was seen to be a complete waste of money. There was lots of hostility from the general public I think in Manchester, but certainly the leadership of the council were very supportive and very keen to actually set up the gay centre.'

Officers in the council who were 'morally opposed' tried to derail the build by suggesting that a £40,000 security system would be needed, but John Clegg, Chair of the Gay Men's Subcommittee, saw through this tactic. However, as Terry Waller recalls, various pressures led to £30,000 being shaved from the budget at the last minute, so plans had to be scaled back – there was no second floor and the quality of the furnishings and fittings was compromised, as generations of centre users can testify!

'About ten members of the church around the corner [King's Church] ... came to the Planning Committee in the Council Chamber at the Town Hall, and all stood up and talked and objected on the grounds that their young people would be whatever, corrupted and damaged... and the councillors as a Planning Committee listened to the public – anybody can speak. There were journalists, members of the public, it's quite a scene, and I've only got one volunteer, Peter [Dungey], and me. But the Council were solid and voted it through. Yes there was opposition from a hell of a lot of Tory media in the run up to it and the planning of it over about a year, including many, many nights when the Evening News' letters page was dominated at times by letters opposing it, but part of my job was to campaign to get letters defending... But apart from that meeting at Planning Committee there's never been a problem with the King's Church people, that I know of anyway. So yes, it was quite a campaign.'

There had been a great deal of talk about building a separate lesbian centre, but securing Sidney Street had been such an undertaking that activists agreed it would have to become the Lesbian and Gay Centre, and serve both. Graham Stringer opened the building. Then, remembers Nigel leach, began the reality of working out how to provide a properly inclusive community service:

'I do remember when we first moved here from Bloom Street it was a giant leap in terms of space, was a giant leap in terms of funding and it was a significant move because it brought being a gay centre and the services that were associated with it into mainstream funding. ...This building was a significant turning point. Yes, it wasn't as big as we'd planned, and the limited space caused some rivalry, but it was a major step forward.'

The centre's significance was recognised during a small group discussion at one of the project's Memory Days:

'Part of the significance of the gay centre is the symbolic value, how many people actually still say, said, "Well I never used to go to gay centre, or very rarely or didn't really access the service, but the fact that it was there meant something." The fact that the Council funded it in the face of opposition, that was important.'

LESBIAN AND GAY CENTRE: SIDNEY STREET - 1990S

Once at Sidney Street the Switchboard created Stepping Stones, a meeting group especially for women. Nigel Leach recalls the centre's attempts to redress the gender imbalance:

Support for Lesbian and Gay Centre, circa 1989

'At the time of moving in we were probably on the old style, mainly gay men's issues ...That's one strand that I vividly remember – lots of conversations around working with people's attitudes, about inclusivity and about diversity and about making our services more open. I think first of all it was moving it from a male-dominated gay centre to involve more women ... and helping people get involved at all levels, so there wasn't an elite of men at the top running things, which is effectively what you probably had at the very beginning.'

A management committee was created with representatives from the different organisations, and people who were there remember this being a hard job, with untrained volunteers having to take difficult decisions and assume serious responsibility.

'By the end of the 1980s there was a greater expectation of what the quality and standards of the services offered would be. There was a pressure (on mostly volunteers) to provide a quality service. The wider sector was experiencing the beginning of professionalisation. There was a contradiction in the level of funding received compared to what was expected of it. ... what we did with minimal means was massive. We were running services and groups, stretching our limited budget, but we were very aware of the need.'

Youth clubs have run at Sidney Street on Tuesday evening and Saturday afternoon continuously since 1988. Lesbian and Gay Youth Manchester (LGYM) got into its stride in the 1990s, with more trained sessional youth workers on the team and more young people involved in running things. Sally Carr was a volunteer at the centre and later became a paid member of staff:

'We lobbied the local authority for my post and then for my colleague [Gordon] who's also been here for a very long time for his post. So we then could offer more time and skill to developing what was at that time Gay Youth Manchester and became Lesbian and Gay Youth Manchester. And then from there we were able to develop other aspects of the work, so we developed the Young Women's Health Project, a very successful project for young lesbians, young bisexual women, young trans* women. We set up a big project called the Peer Support Project in about 1996 and that ran till about 2005.'

In 1995 a volunteer at the centre was charged with a criminal offence, and the way this was handled led to a fall out with the Council and the removal of the grant for the paid worker. It also strained relations between groups and caused the collapse of the management committee, who felt the worker had acted unilaterally in his response to the incident. It fell to council officers and volunteers to keep the place going.

There was a gradual and partial reinstatement of funding at Sidney Street over the next two years, but things were about to shift again. Since the AIDS crisis the health sector had been attracting most funding, prompting talks about a productive merger between Switchboard and Healthy Gay Manchester (HGM). In 2000, Switchboard moved out to join HGM at Ducie House near Piccadilly, forming the Lesbian and Gay Foundation (LGF). Some of the Sidney Street volunteers left to take up paid jobs there.

LGBT CENTRE: SIDNEY STREET - THE 'NOUGHTIES'

In 2000, the Council decided it would prefer to have one organisation overseeing the centre at Sidney Street, rather than a committee. In 2000 they funded Lesbian Community Project (LCP), the successor to Lesbian Link, to take on this role, in addition to catering to the needs and interests of, in particular, older and disabled lesbian women. Most of the other organisations and projects now based at the centre were focussed on young people – Peer Support, Young Women's Health Project, LGYM – but the door had always been open (at least metaphorically – it was often kept locked, making the centre physically hard to access!) to grassroots groups and societies.

One was the monthly Queer Luncheon or 'Quencheon' started by Sylvia Kölling and Kim Foale in 2008. It had a similar ethos to Kaffequeeria which ran from 2004 - 2009 and was set up by three organisers of Ladyfest Manchester 2003 - Humaira Saeed, Clare Tebbutt and Heena Patel. The Kaffequeeria collective grew over the years, organising queer cafes, workshops, gigs and discos with a feminist do-it-yourself ethos, and founded the alternative pride event Get Bent! in 2005.

Sylvia explains that she organised the 'Quencheon' because:

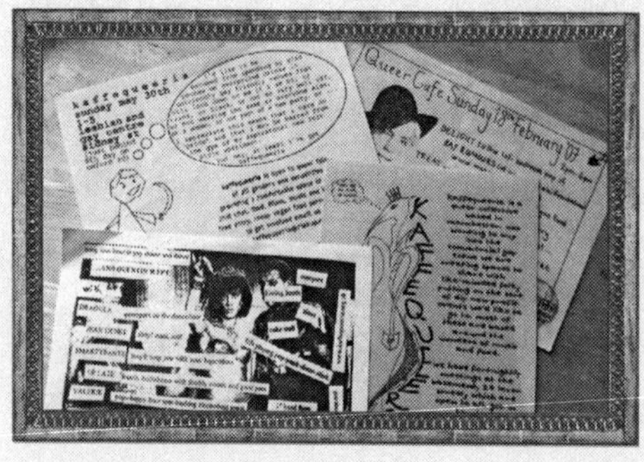

Publicity for Queer Luncheon or 'Quencheon' and Kaffequeeria, Sylvia Kölling 2009

'We got frustrated with the lack of provisions for specifically queer people, not LGBT because there's a lot there for LGBT. And decided to do a day time thing for people with little or no money, once a month, where they can just come and not get drunk … .So we would come in, use the kitchen, cook something, open at 12, close at four or five-ish depending on how many people were there. We sold badges, accepted donations, and it was actually quite nice. We had anything from three to 15 people depending on the time of year, and the weather. We ran that for about four years, and then called it quits.'

Sylvia remembers appreciating it when the 'male and female toilets' became the more gender-neutral 'cubicles and urinals'. Sidney Street had the inclusive LGBT moniker by this point, and trans* groups such as Morph were using it for meetings. Jenny-Anne Bishop also enjoyed the transgenerational aspect of the Sunday café:

'We used to have little leaflets with Quencheon on and we advertised it in our trans* things, and my partner Ellen and I nearly always on a Sunday come into Manchester to go to church at half past four in Chorlton. And quite often we'd say, "Well let's go and have Queer Lunch," and we come and we'd join the young people, and we'd have a really nice lunch, very low cost, and also it helped us to stay grounded with what the young people were doing. You know, because if you want to understand the community you need to keep talking to the people who are really in the community, not just those who think they know about it!'

As always the financial situation was precarious. Sylvia Kölling recalled awkward, bulky furniture and that negotiating the kitchen became "adventurous" when the Council closed it down:

'We'd bring our own pots and pans because there was just not enough equipment. And for about a year we didn't have hot water, so we'd just bring our own stuff and then wash up at home – dishes was a really sore issue because a lot of user groups would either not do their dishes, or not put them away, so we would find the kitchen in all sorts of states! Then for the last year or two we'd have to climb through the window and open the door... I think the boiler had broken and they'd just closed the kitchen entirely, but the shutters weren't locked, so you could just pull the shutters up and climb through, then undo the lock.'

Towards the end of its second term, the New Labour government was gripped by a fervour for mainstreaming specialist services, which found favour locally with the council's lead member for lesbian issues, Mary Murphy. She wanted the centre closed down, as interviewees from one of the project's Memory Days discussed:

'... rather than hiding ourselves in an LGBT building, hiding away from the world, the users of this building need to get out in the world, being integrated. It's the old line about it'd be a success when you don't need your gay village anymore.'

The successful campaign which was galvanised against closure had to be reprieved in 2010 when the Council announced sweeping cuts (including the total axing of the Youth Service) in the wake of the election of the Coalition government. Myrtle Finley recalls:

'We were told that the centre was going to close so we had to be out of there by December. ... the council were going to sell it off, and so things had to shut down. And everyone was just like, "This can't happen!"... We stood our ground really, people who had been involved in the centre from the very beginning or who'd accessed the different youth groups and so on came and spoke out so there was, you know, a big campaign – petition, a kind of campaign on social media, we had a big public meeting where people from the council came down, listened to people's stories. Parents came, young people. It was packed and we kept the space open, you know. It really showed how people can come together and that kind of collective community spirit can really be used to keep things alive and to actually stop things... stop negative things from happening... And we were able to show that... they realised they couldn't close it, it couldn't be closed because it was such a vital thing in the community, yeah.'

Joyce Layland, activist and one of the founders of Manchester Parents Group, representing Manchester Gay Centre, alongside Peter Cookson

JOYCE LAYLAND LGBT CENTRE - 2010 AND BEYOND!

In 2012 LCP lost its funding and was wound up, but the long term youth workers at Sidney Street were prepared. They had seen the writing on the wall and had set up LGBT Youth North West as an independent charitable company, which was ready to step in and

Groups using the centre in 2014:
Lesbian and Gay Youth Manchester,
Trans Youth - Afternoon TEA (Trans Education & Action),
Young Women's Group, Edward Carpenter Community,
Rainbow Noir, SM Dykes, Narcotics Anonymous,
Alcoholics Anonymous,
University of Manchester LGBTQ Society,
Parents of Trans Children Group,
Lesbian Immigration Support Group

assume the running of the centre. Myrtle Finley is astutely aware of the need for those who look after and manage the centre to find alternative ways of resourcing it:

'It used to have a lot more support from the council. It was one of their buildings, so they would maintain it and fund it ... [Now the] public sector cuts and moves for public buildings to be taken over privately has meant that the LGBT Centre has had to look at creating its own kind of business plan and its own way of getting other resourcing in.'

In 2010, the centre was dedicated to long-time activist Joyce Layland, who had recently died. A desire to have more Manchester buildings honouring local women outweighed a few doubts about singling out one individual from such a fundamentally collective enterprise.

A library created in partnership with 42nd Street's Young Women's Health Project, originally spanning both sites and called Between the Lines, was also renamed in memory

Right: The Jaye Bloomfield Resource Library, with thanks to Nicolas Chinardet photography

of a centre supporter, Jaye Bloomfield, in 2013. Amelia Lee sees these moves perhaps reflecting the gender rebalancing that has occurred over the centre's 26 years.

'Although there's many different groups that meet here it predominantly is the women's space, the youth space, the trans* space and that's the gap that it plugs in the mix, really, which has changed over time, hasn't it, substantially.'

LGBT Youth North West reinstated a centre-user group committee to give the other user groups a stake in the running of the centre, and to try to avoid it being perceived as 'just' a youth centre. This building is accessible to many groups within the community, and while the youth group is an important feature, the centre has a community feel which activists have worked hard to create. The longstanding 'exclusive use' culture has been maintained – on the nights or mornings when Alcoholics Anonymous, Rainbow Noir or the Edward Carpenter Society, for example, are meeting, they can expect to have the building to themselves.

The major recent innovation has been opening of Sidney Street Café in 2013, following refurbishment and a kitchen retrofit thanks to money from the Co-operative and various small trusts. Part of the long term financial sustainability plan, this mainly vegetarian lunchtime café has brought new life to the centre, whose door, Sylvia Kölling tells us, is now opened wide to the street during the day:

'I know a lot of people just thought it was a youth centre … it still has that kind of feel to it in a way, but it's much nicer now. And I think a lot of people will get a better idea when they come and actually eat in the café and look around, and see what it says on the signs and stuff. So it seems much more open now.'

The Joyce Layland LGBT Centre, Sidney Street, 2014

Looking to the future, Sidney Street may well get its second floor at some point, possibly even a third, if ideas for a specialist unit for LGBT young people not in mainstream education come to fruition. Once pretty much the only place in Manchester where young LGBT people felt safe to hang out, the centre now operates in a much wider context of provision, and has become somewhere for people to come and explore their identities, rather than just somewhere to escape to.

The Bloom Street Gay Centre's first worker, Paul Fairweather, describes "huge changes in legislation and attitude" since his initial days:

'I think you couldn't have predicted how much things have changed, and how it has changed really. And I think it's important that, you know, there are places for a whole range of people to go, different, you know, different venues. The thing about here is a lot of very small support groups actually use it and feel safe using it here, which I think is really important. You've now got the LGF (a big centre right in the village) and a whole range of groups meet there as well. So there's much more choice for people, a lot of other opportunities, there's lots of other resources. You've got The Albert Kennedy Trust, you've got George House Trust, the LGBT voluntary sector in Manchester is very big so there's lots and lots of places to meet. And I think it's a lot easier, in some ways for lots of young people to come out, it's a lot easier to be gay. There's a debate about, you know, are gay centres needed, do you need to gay village, do you need the gay centre? And I think we still do, but I think the situation is very different than it was 20, 30, 40 years ago.'

Throughout its different incarnations, the LGBT centre has offered people community, friendship and even relationships. Several interviewees talked of meeting short and long term partners during meetings! It has offered political apprenticeships; formal and informal skills training; opportunities to innovate and the satisfaction of "giving something back". For many, such as Nigel Leach and Sarah Gilston respectively, it unexpectedly launched their careers.

'There have been any number of people who've made a massive contribution over the years to maintaining the services which were largely voluntary, you know, a massive involvement. And again, running a set of services like that, the volunteers themselves have said things like, how [it] made a big difference to their own lifestyle, enriching it ... being gay wasn't just about going out and meeting people in bars and clubs ... it's a lifestyle based on making a positive contribution and making a difference with people who'd had similar difficulties. ... Motivated people, when they saw a gap, went out there to advocate and campaign for bits of funding to go and do stuff that actually was creating new things.'

'I came along to the centre being like 24, 25 ... too old to be involved as a young person but, you know, that's how I got involved in volunteering here. Which then eventually led to working, and then I didn't leave for seven years! I fell into youth work, and so it just felt like a nurturing environment where you felt you had a real input into what was going on … people could make suggestions which you don't really get in a lot of work places.'

And because of the meaningful nature of the work, people have tended to stick around for some time, providing a continuity which has enabled it to develop and withstand many crises. Myrtle Finley was one of many who appreciated the centre:

'It was a really safe space, that it was inclusive of different identities and that's really important. And I think that's sadly quite rare, because people talk about LGBT but actually a lot of the time they think lesbian and gay, they don't think of the kind of inclusive spectrum of sexual orientation and gender identity, and the other needs people have which they do here. So that that's why the centre has been and still is a massive thing for me as well.'

According to Paul Fairweather's recollections:

'The London Lesbian and Gay Centre was set up before this one, set up with far more money, but it didn't actually work due to in-fighting, I think, and there was a gay centre in Chester, in Preston. Birmingham had a big gay centre before this one in Manchester. But actually I think there's something about Manchester - a combination of very strong LGBT community, the gay village, and a very supportive council. This is the only purpose-built LGBT centre in this country certainly, it's the only one that's actually been built by the council, in that sense.'

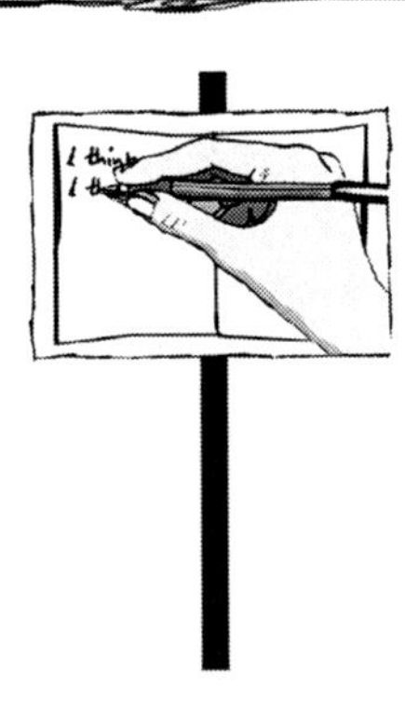

How does Manchester fit in?

London, Chester, Preston, Birmingham – were there any other gay centres in UK cities and towns before the 1990s?

There are lots of LGBT history sites on the web - what can you find out?

What do you or your friends know?

Did others evolve in a similar way, with help lines, campaigners and volunteers deciding to get together under one roof?

Did other centres receive local authority grants, or was Manchester indeed unique?

CHAPTER 8

ACTING UP AND ACTING OUT

AMELIA LEE

'LGBT Youth North West and the LGBT youth groups mean a future for LGBT youth. Somewhere where they can come when their minds are in turmoil, and someone will put an arm round them and say, "It's okay, that's what we're here for".'
Barbara Spence, Manchester Parents Group.

This chapter is about youth work with LGBT young people, the youth workers and supporters who have helped make that youth work happen, and the impact it has had on people's lives. The focus is on Manchester and the North West, which reflect in many ways the wider UK story.

Young people from Lesbian and Gay Youth Manchester (LGYM) on a residential trip in the 1990s

BEGINNINGS ...

In the same way that much of the history in this book is messy, it is not clear exactly when LGBT youth work emerged, or rather gay youth work (the LB and T came after). Although LGBT people had been in youth groups and clubs ever since the start of organised youth work (The Boys Brigade in 1883, The Scouts in 1908, the Girl Guides in 1909), they were usually not able to be "out" in those spaces. There were legal and cultural reasons for this, for example sex between men being illegal until 1967 in the UK, and the cultural expectation that young women should find a man, get married to him, have children and be the home-maker.

So it is probably accurate to assume that gay youth groups began to emerge when the gay civil rights movements in the UK began (which helped bring about the law change in 1967), and was spurred on by the civil rights of LGBT people in America (marked by the Stonewall Riots in 1969).

Youth Work is working with young people in an environment of informal education. It uses lots of specific methods (including group work techniques such as cooperative games) and is guided by some key principles which make it much more than just activities for young people. These are:

- Focusing on young people, their needs, experiences and contribution (commonly known as 'starting where a young person is at').
- Voluntary participation, young people choose to become involved in the work.
- Fostering association, relationship and community, encouraging all to join in friendship, to organise and take part in groups and activities and deepen and develop relationships and that allow them to grow and flourish.
- Being friendly, accessible and responsive while acting with integrity. Youth work has come to be characterized by a belief that workers should not only be approachable and friendly; but also that they should have faith in people; and be trying, themselves, to live good lives.
- Looking to the education and, more broadly, the whole young person's entire welfare.
- Challenging discrimination and oppression, and supporting young people to do the same.

Adapted from Jeffs and Smith's book *Youth Work (1987)*

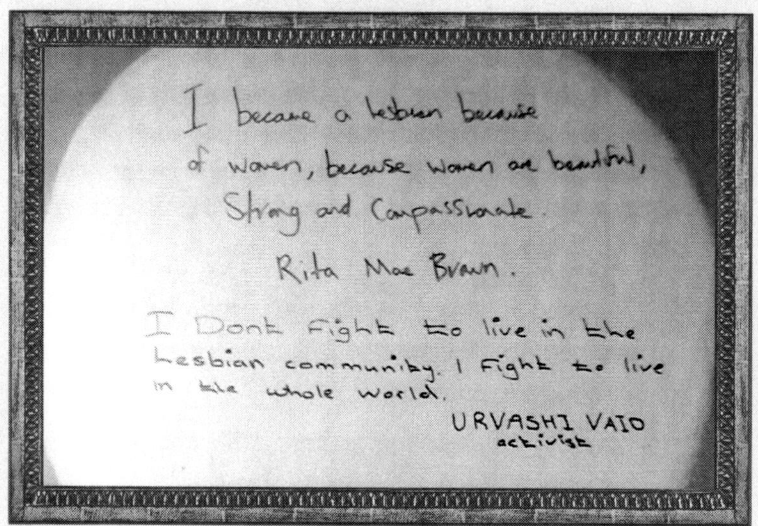

From the early days of meeting in rooms above bars, youth groups started to become more visible and organised from the 1970s onward. Liverpool, Manchester and London were some of the first places to have gay youth groups, though it is hard to track exactly where each group emerged and when, because they were begun very informally by groups of volunteers – which is precisely why projects like this book are important, to document these hidden histories.

It is also interesting to track the rise of lesbian visibility in the feminist movement during the same era, and how many lesbian feminists ‘fell into youth work’ as a way of putting their politics into action. In the youth work field they not only became active in running and supporting LGBT youth groups, but also in ensuring that mixed groups had a stronger and more positive ethos around inclusion and diversity. This included LGBT young people, as well as inclusion for young people who were black, disabled, young mothers and others who were stigmatised in society. One such youth worker was Jayne Mugglestone:

‘I think youth work is right up my street, ’cause it’s informal and it’s really clued up on politics really, and kind of an “ever left”, definitely a left wing socialist perspective, which is completely me. And there’s loads of freedom to sort

Above: Quotes written in the toilet of the Joyce Layland LGBT Centre

p.127 Key moments 1970s to early 1990s, diagram by Amelia Lee

Key moments that affected LGBT Youth Work History

1970s: out of the women's liberation movement comes Girls Work as a space for young women to get together to challenge stereotypes, and discrimination

In the 1970s, The Gay Liberation Front lays out a manifesto of what gay people deserve

In the 1980s, anti-Section 28 campaigning called Never Going Underground helps bond LGBT youth groups across England and Wales

In the 1980s and 1990s the HIV and AIDS epidemic kills hundreds of gay men, but the LGBT community unites in support

Some key impact of these key events on youth work

Some of the Girls Work youth workers got the courage to come out, and helped run LGBT youth groups

Manchester, London and Liverpool volunteers start Gay Youth Groups in the 1970s. Mostly people aged 19-27 attend

The Gay Centre volunteers in Manchester, and other groups (such is in London) form switchboards, including youth helplines

Lesbian and Gay youth groups begin to grow around the country, including in towns and smaller areas the North West and Yorkshire e.g. Wigan, Calderdale, Newcastle

of be who you are. So in any youth work I've done and seen, people have always been really good at empowering, and they've understood things like racism and sexism and homophobia and all that kind of stuff. If you'd said to me I was going to be a teacher, I'd have really struggled. I'd have struggled with looking smart, and I suppose, what I would have struggled with was the heterosexuality of it. And I didn't know when I first started doing youth work that I was going to come out!'

There were many events in the wider social and political sphere that influenced the development of LGBT youth work. Peter Cookson, who was young person attending the Manchester Gay Youth Group in the 1980s and is now a local Councillor, talks about why people did, and still do, need LGBT youth groups:

'In the 1980s people still thought it was a disease, an affliction, a mental illness. People were sending their kids away for treatment even though, by then, it wasn't legal to do that anymore. So the youth group was a safe space, an outlet, and we needed that.'

Many of the people we interviewed talked about growing up feeling that fancying someone of the same sex was isolating and scary. Many people didn't have words like gay, lesbian or bisexual to identify themselves, and grew up thinking they were the only one who felt that way.

"SO THE YOUTH GROUP WAS A SAFE SPACE, AN OUTLET, AND WE NEEDED THAT."

PETER COOKSON

When people decided to come out, many faced ridicule, violence, police harassment and even, in some cases, murder (sometimes at the hand of 'gay-bashers' on the streets and even their own family).

Thankfully some parents were supportive of their children, and when their children came out, they wanted to help them meet other people like them. This was the case for people such as Barbara Spence who was just one of the many parents who supported setting up LGBT youth groups, and volunteered in them, to help their children make friends, and not face being outsiders:

"THE GREAT THING ABOUT THE YOUTH CLUB WAS THAT THERE WERE YOUNG PEOPLE WHO WEREN'T OUT ELSEWHERE. IT WAS THE ONLY PLACE THEY HAD."

PETER COOKSON

'I didn't have a problem with it, I just wanted to know more… every community had the local gay, you know, the gay in the village, and the one I knew from Wigan was a right shifty character, and I thought, "dear God, if my son turns out like that, what am I going to do?"'

Youth groups began as very informal. Volunteers (parents or adult LGBT people) delivered the sessions and they usually did not have any youth work training. What they did have was a passion for helping, so they just got stuck in. They knew for many who came along, like Peter Cookson, that it was the only place they could be themselves.

'The great thing about the youth club was that there were young people who weren't out anywhere else. It was the only place they had.'

As the groups developed over time, they became part of the professionalization of youth work from the 1980s onwards. They adopted some of the principles of youth work, such as young people and staff having more of an equal say about what would be happening in the groups. They wanted to make it a more empowering space, though some groups found this harder than others.

2006 LGBT Youth Workers Network

2011 LGBT youth workers residential

In 2014, LGBT Youth North West interviewed 128 young LGBT people to ask them how they would like adults to support them in their lives, and to give feedback on what has been good or bad about adults' interactions with them.
Less than 25% felt they had a supportive adult to turn to in their lives. Many were facing rejection by families and by religions they belonged to; ridicule at school; and a personal feeling of isolation. What came through very strongly though, was their positive relationships with youth workers and the difference youth workers had made to them, as the findings from LGBT Youth North West's 2014 research 'How You Can Help Us' shows.

'I don't know what it is … But youth workers just understand us more. They're always prepared to talk and listen, and signpost. I think their knowledge is what makes the difference for me.
Youth workers are more supportive of me than my parents, and I see them for an hour a week. I feel safe, and like they understand what I'm going through.'

Lots of young people have to pluck the courage up to attend their first LGBT youth group, some even saying they had to walk around the block six times before getting themselves through the door! That is as true now as it was back in the 1970s and 1980s:

WHAT MAKES YOUTH WORK SPECIAL?

Young people who felt on the edges of mainstream society and rarely accepted and understood in their school or family, found in their youth groups the community and family that they needed, a sense of association, a sense of belonging, and where they felt accepted, not in spite of who they were, but for exactly who they were. Sally Carr M.B.E has been a youth worker for over 25 years and explains why she always will be:

'You know, youth work, one of the values is starting where the young people are at and that makes you always reconsider where the young people are at, the things that are going on in their lives right now, and you only get that sense through conversations, so it's important to be grounded and to keep in touch. Why I will always be a youth worker is because of the humour of the young people and their ability to keep going. They are finding out about themselves and doing something about it, that's incredibly brave. Youth work is about freeing people's hearts and minds so that they can be fully part of the world, not looking on from the side-lines.'

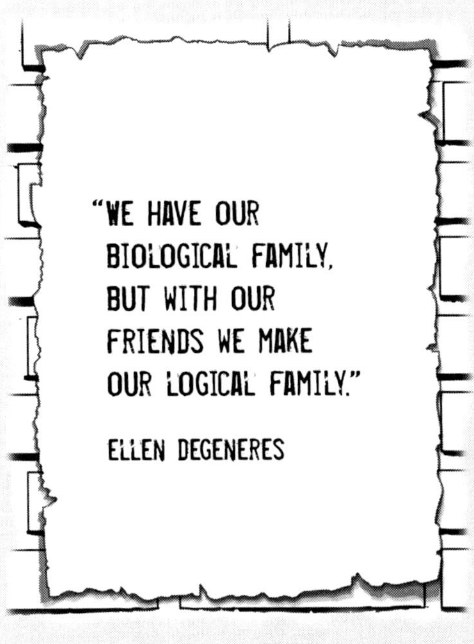

Often what sticks in the minds of young people and youth workers are the trips that they go on. These might be residential trips (also known as residentials or "resies" for short) or day trips. The Manchester Youth Group would visit the London group in the 1980s, and also have day trips out to nice places like the seaside in Blackpool. Lesbian and Gay Youth Manchester (LGYM) would go on to have trips to Amsterdam (the Netherlands), Spain, Germany, and even Canada in the 2000s. In turn Manchester built links with the International Lesbian and Gay Youth Organisation (IGLYO) and in 1995 hosted their international

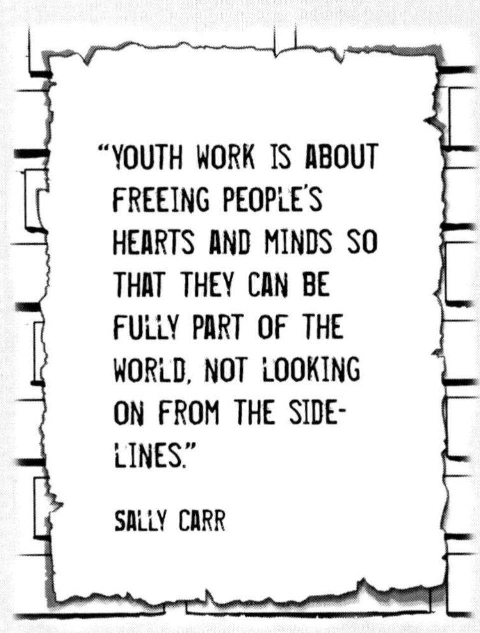

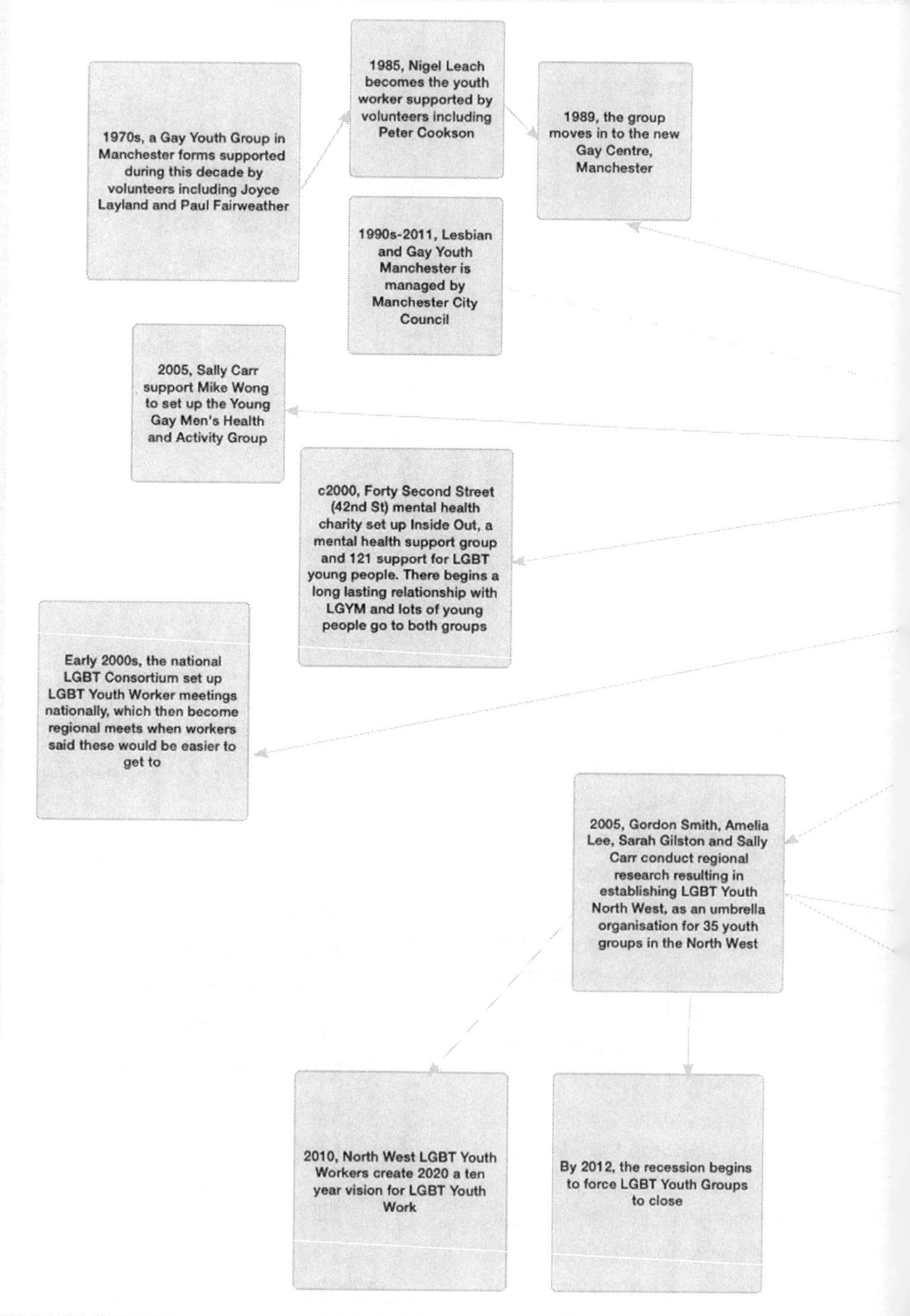

1970s, a Gay Youth Group in Manchester forms supported during this decade by volunteers including Joyce Layland and Paul Fairweather

1985, Nigel Leach becomes the youth worker supported by volunteers including Peter Cookson

1989, the group moves in to the new Gay Centre, Manchester

1990s-2011, Lesbian and Gay Youth Manchester is managed by Manchester City Council

2005, Sally Carr support Mike Wong to set up the Young Gay Men's Health and Activity Group

c2000, Forty Second Street (42nd St) mental health charity set up Inside Out, a mental health support group and 121 support for LGBT young people. There begins a long lasting relationship with LGYM and lots of young people go to both groups

Early 2000s, the national LGBT Consortium set up LGBT Youth Worker meetings nationally, which then become regional meets when workers said these would be easier to get to

2005, Gordon Smith, Amelia Lee, Sarah Gilston and Sally Carr conduct regional research resulting in establishing LGBT Youth North West, as an umbrella organisation for 35 youth groups in the North West

2010, North West LGBT Youth Workers create 2020 a ten year vision for LGBT Youth Work

By 2012, the recession begins to force LGBT Youth Groups to close

LGYM's History - Created in 'Ideas Sketch' by Amelia Lee

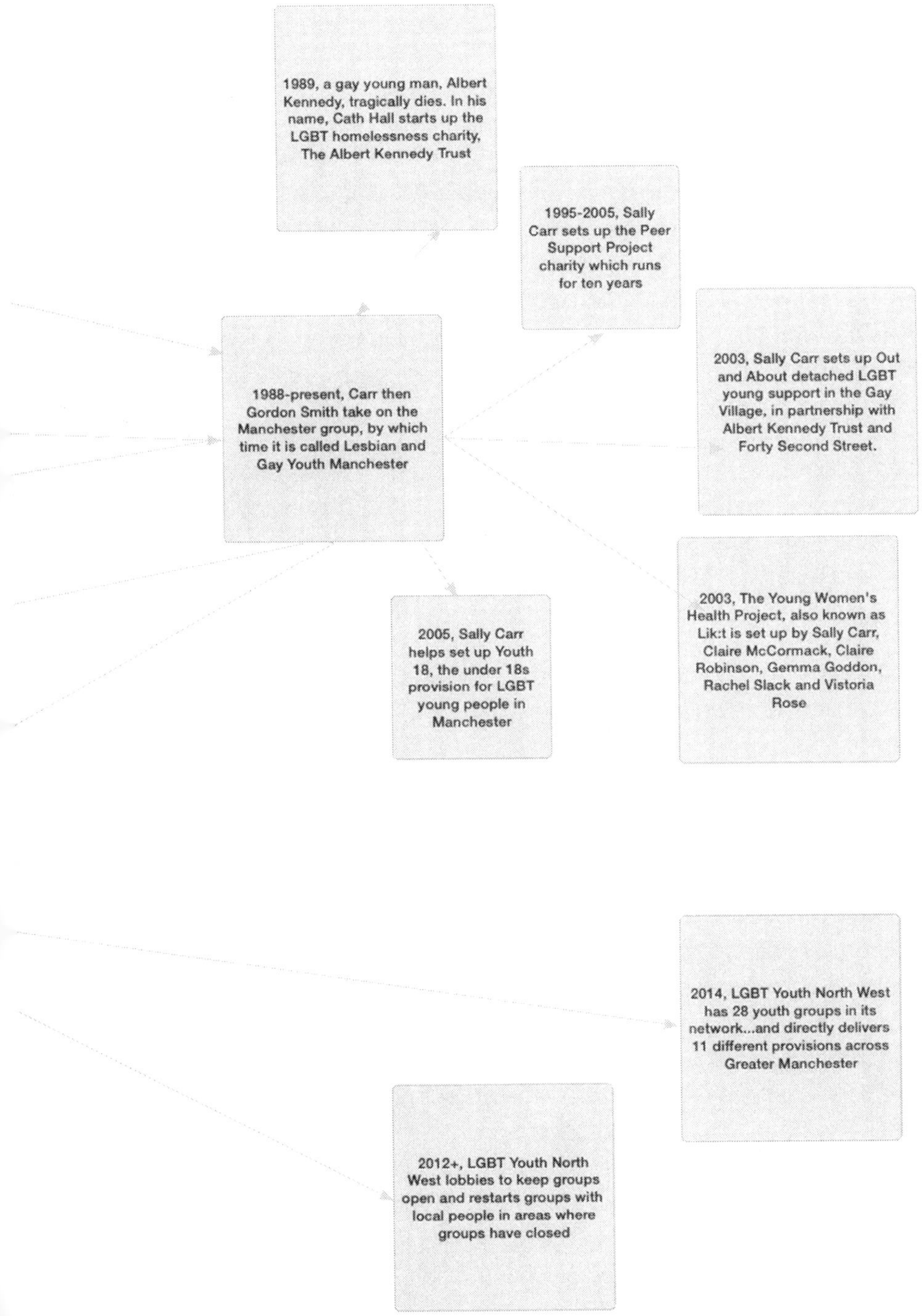

1989, a gay young man, Albert Kennedy, tragically dies. In his name, Cath Hall starts up the LGBT homelessness charity, The Albert Kennedy Trust

1995-2005, Sally Carr sets up the Peer Support Project charity which runs for ten years

2003, Sally Carr sets up Out and About detached LGBT young support in the Gay Village, in partnership with Albert Kennedy Trust and Forty Second Street.

1988-present, Carr then Gordon Smith take on the Manchester group, by which time it is called Lesbian and Gay Youth Manchester

2003, The Young Women's Health Project, also known as Lik:t is set up by Sally Carr, Claire McCormack, Claire Robinson, Gemma Goddon, Rachel Slack and Vistoria Rose

2005, Sally Carr helps set up Youth 18, the under 18s provision for LGBT young people in Manchester

2014, LGBT Youth North West has 28 youth groups in its network...and directly delivers 11 different provisions across Greater Manchester

2012+, LGBT Youth North West lobbies to keep groups open and restarts groups with local people in areas where groups have closed

Conference, with people visiting from many other countries, at which they prepared messages for the United Nations Women's Conference in Beijing.

For groups that live in smaller towns or more rural areas, a highlight of the calendar was and is going to a Pride celebration. Pride is a get together of LGBT people to campaign and celebrate their identity. Manchester's precursor to Pride was a jumble sale-style event in the mid-1980s held to raise money during the HIV and AIDS crisis. From the late 1980s a Pride event began, which developed a parade element to show LGBT visibility throughout the city. This is now watched by thousands of people, and visitors come from across the world to participate in Pride. Therese Downham is youth worker at the BYoU LGBT youth group in Wigan and attended a pride event with young people:

'When it comes to Pride, you watch their faces and, I know one male said to me once, "Everybody's photographing me. I can't believe the amount of people that have photographed me. I must be in everybody's camera!" …you know, and that was really good. It was something like, "woah!" you know. And another thing about Pride is they feel accepted: it's their Christmas.'

Manchester's youth group history intertwines with regional and national LGBT youth work history, which we have shown here in this relationship map on pages 132/133.

School education is a legal (statutory) responsibility in the UK, so all children have to go to school by law. Youth work is not a legal requirement so young people can choose to go to a youth club or not. Youth work, therefore, often sits on the margins as a profession, and is not well understood outside of the profession. Perhaps it is also undervalued because it doesn't have the status of being fully 'professional', because not everyone who is a youth worker has received a qualification in it. One youth worker who started as a volunteer at LGYM, Elaina Quesada, and who is now qualified, reflects that "many youth workers feel that it is precisely the semi-professional nature of youth work that still gives it the space to do good work". Rather than treating young people like a number and processing them through a compulsory system of exams, youth workers can work with young people in a more holistic, informal way. Youth workers have had to fight against a system that moved them away from empowering, edgy work and into so-called "tick box" exercises, as Alison Ronan explains:

'I think through the late '80s and the '90s things got much harder. There were a lot more things about whether young people had been assessed and achieved certain targets. All this kind of stuff that was going on, and I suppose under the New Labour project that didn't change very much. It had a lot of plausibility, I mean, you feel that with this word 'accountability', which didn't exist I don't think in the 1970s. Of course we do need to be accountable for the money we spend but what I don't like is that it sometimes affects the way in which the work is done if that makes sense. Does it?'

In 2014, a group of adults who had attended Lesbian and Gay Youth Manchester in the 1990s asked Sally Carr, their former youth worker, to run a re-union for them. During this day she asked them some questions about how the group had affected their lives. The now "grown-up" LGYM members reflect on their youth and the impact of the youth group:

'When I was 18 I saw an advert on [local] TV for LGYM. Until that moment I had no idea how I was going to meet other gay people. LGYM gave me a network of friends, gave me the courage to stand up out and proud to ... bigotry and prejudice but more importantly to find myself.'

'Knowing I wasn't alone. Meeting people my own age who were going through similar situations. Acceptance for who I was regardless of what you looked like/social situation. Self-confidence, more proactive about speaking out against discrimination. Feel safe.'

'Gave me confidence to face the world and be proud of who I am.'

'Empower my self-identity, help to put down ideas of shame, disgust etc. with

respect to your sexuality.'

'At a very scary and lonely time, I found friends, family and a place in society.'

'It made me empowered & wiser (of the variety of people in the world not in an Einstein kinda way) it also gave me some wonderful people who are still in my life.'

'Educated me about… peer pressure & equality, which has resulted in me getting more involved in workplace trade unions.'

'Relationships with peers. Acceptance from peers.'

'Confidence. I was very quiet but coming here gave me a voice and the confidence to use it.'

'From my first meeting … I realised that I'm not a freak or unnatural, it's ok to be me. It got enforced each week and got stronger and stronger.'

'It's good to see how people have grown. Good to see how the group has helped people. It shows how support networks are always there and are always accessible.'

'I remember the group for sore knees, laughs, smiles and memories.'

'It made us all well rounded individuals not a representative of the "gay scene" necessarily, I think we are more balanced. Largely through workers at LGYM such as Sally [Carr] and Gordon [Smith].'

'It gives me a family feeling, understanding, warm, safe.'

'It taught me that you should not change yourself for anyone but you.'

'I learnt about the gay community, to stand on my own two feet, and learning that I can be my own champion.'

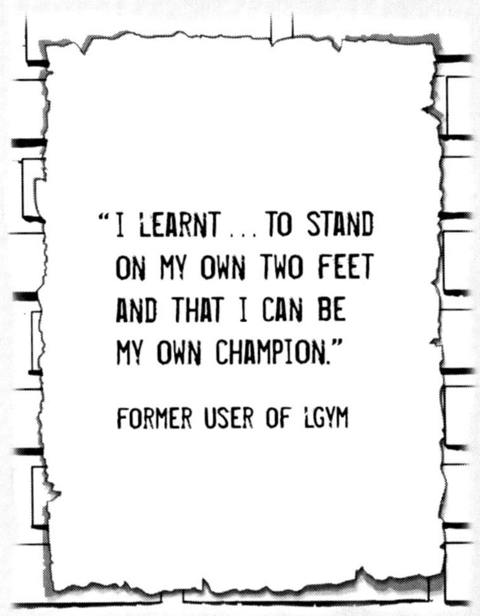

'Sometimes you have to realize that you can't change someone's viewpoint even if you have logic, intelligence and morals on your side, because people are not always accepting.'

Advice that the now "grown-up" LGYM members would give to their 18 year old selves:

'Don't do anything now that you'd be ashamed of in the future.'

'Take a chance.'

'Sex isn't everything.'

'Stop going out every night.'

'You'll be ok. You are attractive. Cut your hair!'

'Don't worry what people think.'

'Don't worry about the little things. If there is any negative people in your life get rid of them, there's millions of people in the world.'

'Don't close your emotions off.'

'Make more of an effort to keep in touch!'

'Just don't worry about things – they always sort themselves out and worry changes nothing.'

'Treat people how you would like to be treated.'

In 2008, Mike Wong thanked LGYM on their 30th anniversary in this speech:

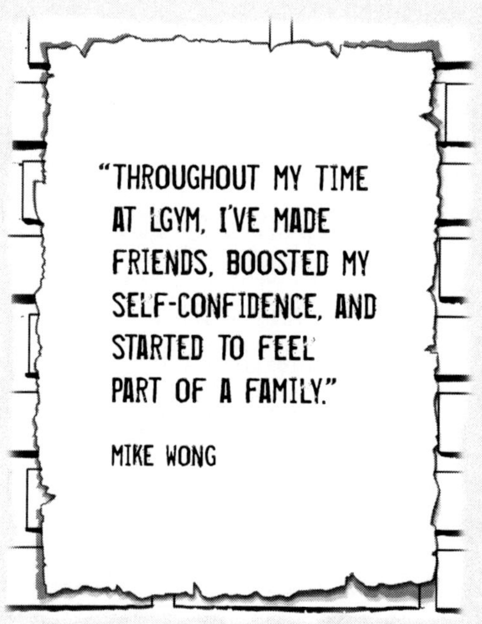

'I first attended LGYM when I was 22. Very unsure of myself, didn't have anyone to identify myself with and lacking in self-esteem. Throughout my time at LGYM, I've made many friends, boosted my self-confidence, and started to feel part of a family. Through LGYM, I've been to many places, met loads of really interesting and diverse people, but most of all, felt comfortable in a safe and supportive environment. Thank you Lesbian and Gay Youth Manchester.'

Andy attended LGYM for many years throughout the 1990s:

'I was kicked out of the family home at fifteen for being gay and subsequently spent the following few years in a haze of drink, drugs, prostitution and general self-destruction. Then in 1997, I arrived back in Manchester and was being treated in a recovery centre. They wanted me to go to this gay youth group on a Saturday to start mixing with other people my own age well away from a pub. I wasn't too keen on the idea but they said it had free coffee and biscuits, so that was it. If my memory's correct, I think they'd been doing kite-making and I arrived at the end of the session. It seemed a friendly group but it still took a few weeks for to start talking to people beyond a few grunts. Over the following years however, Sidney Street became my second home and Sally, Gordon and the group, my surrogate family.

Through the silly games and outdoor activities, I learnt how to laugh again and have fun whilst sober. It also gave me a chance to try things like kayaking I otherwise wouldn't have been able to afford. Through the workshops I learnt how to understand and process my issues and I had others to talk to and share experiences with. My confidence started to grow, my self-esteem appeared and for the first time in years I started making friends.

Through LGYM I got involved with the Peer Support Project (PSP), which grew out of LGYM, helping on the Youthline, Postal Support and 1-2-1 Befriending

Scheme. To do this we had the training residential trips, team building activities etc. These helped show me that I had real skills and was capable of doing things, which gave me a real sense of worth.

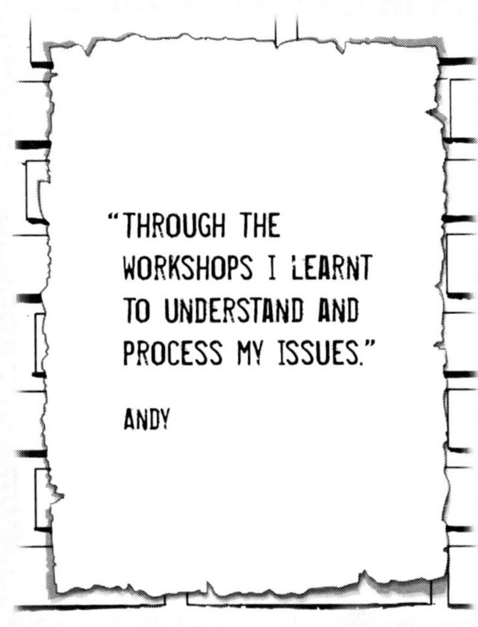

I was lucky enough to be able to do my Prince's Trust placement at LGYM/ PSP and learnt to facilitate workshops, plan sessions and had to organise a Boys Health Day event inviting other youth groups, and produce the project's magazine. Because of my work there, I was taken on in my first proper job at the Princes Trust as an Assistant Team Leader.

Over the years the help, support, advice and friendships I've received from LGYM has turned me into a confident, calmer person with a lot of skills to fall back on. It's no surprise how many of us have chosen to go into youth/ social work. We appreciate how much of an effect good youth work can have on young people.'

Julian Kelly reflects on the relationship between Section 28 and Manchester's Gay Youth Group:

'February of 1988, Kylie Minogue's "I should be so lucky" had just been knocked off five weeks at number one by Azwad. Tensions were already high for a fifteen year old gay boy in a box room in East Didsbury clutching on to a copy of the Gay Times (from a pile of ten hidden under the bed). I had known exactly what gay meant ever since every boy in 2D had burst into laughter as the word gay was read out loud by Miss Dearden from a poem called "Bright and Gay." I had been buying Gay Times since I was 14 from the Cornerhouse shop and avidly reading about the gay goings-on around the country. It was in this magazine that I had read about the horror of Section 28 and the planned rally in Manchester. At this stage I didn't know any other gay people and I

had only come out to my Maltese Terrier. (Years later it surfaced that my Wendy House and Girls World head had given the game away to my family.) I knew I had to attend this rally and that it would become a defining moment for me in so many ways.

On the morning of the rally I put on my best yellow dungarees and boldly got on the 42 into town – telling my mum I was meeting my friend Joanne to go shopping. As I approached the starting point, I was met by the sight of, quite literally, thousands of lesbian and gay people blowing whistles. It was almost too much but I knew it was the gay universe calling me. Desperately trying to look cool I hung around the edge of a group of people. A voice through a loud speaker boomed across the passionate crowd and everyone started to move. An older woman with a shaved head looked round and saw that I was alone. She took me by the hand and said "Come on chicken, you stick with us". Marching along the streets with the press taking photos of us, holding on to an actual gay person's hand for the first time – something awoke in me and I was no longer "One of them" but "One of us". Almost hoarse from joining in with chants of "Two, four, six, eight, is that copper really straight", we got to Albert Square where the march ended. A stage had been put up in front of the town hall where Andy Bell and Jimmy Somerville did a duet and made rousing speeches about "never going underground." I had only ever seen them in my Smash Hits magazine and here they were screaming to me to get proud about myself. I knew I had arrived and that there was no turning back from this. In the space of one day I had become a different person with an improved outlook on the future. Not brave enough to risk a gay bar (until later that year), I went home. By six o'clock I was sat on my sofa with my tea on my knee and I told my mum I had been to Affleck's Palace, not mentioning the rally once.

In the summer of that year, I turned 16, left the hell that was school and I joined Contact Youth Theatre. I did this strategically to make gay friends. My first gay friend was called Becky. It was Becky that first told me about a little gem of friendliness on Sidney Street – the gay centre. The night after a [Contact] Youth Theatre meeting, she took me there and if my memory serves me correctly we had a game of Bingo! There were other 16 year old gay people talking about their life and subsequently my own life starting falling into place. The spring board effect of that year and the people I chatted to at the gay centre have been at my core over the past 26 years. No matter what I've done or survived over the years, a small part of me has always been that teenager in yellow dungarees desperately trying to act like I wasn't out of my depth. I still never let it show when I am.'

In changing times the future of LGBT work may look very different. Here are just a few of the changes that we have noticed:

- LGBT people are coming out at a younger age than they did 30 years ago (average age in 2014 in UK was 15).
- Trans* youth work is a growing area of youth work as more trans* young people come out than in previous years. As a result, in our youth groups we often start the sessions with going around the circle, and everyone saying their name plus their preferred 'gender pronoun' e.g. she, he or they.
- Most people in 2014 find out about their youth group through searching on the internet, which was unheard of 15 years ago.

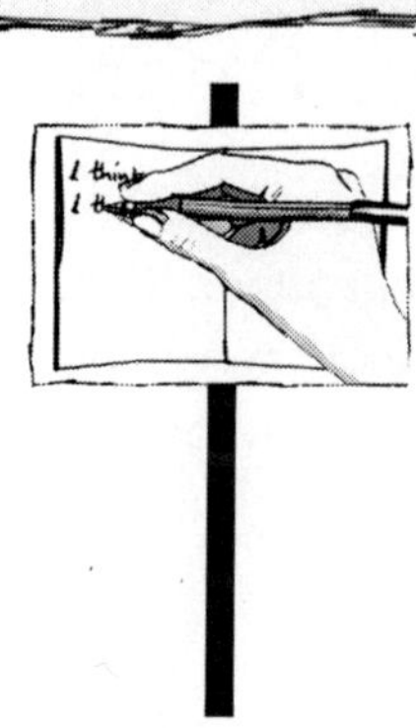

Can you come up with ideas of what you think LGBT youth work should like in the future? Here are a few to start you off …

- An online youth group (like *Sims* or *Second Life*) …
- More LGBT support for Black, Asian, and Roma young people …

Can you draw what your ideal youth club would look like here?

CHAPTER 9

A WOMAN'S PLACE

HEBE PHILIPS

'Lifestyle feminism ushered in the notion that there could be as many versions of feminism as there were women. Suddenly the politics was being slowly removed from feminism. And the assumption prevailed that no matter what a woman's politics, be she conservative or liberal, she too could fit feminism into her existing lifestyle. Obviously this way of thinking has made feminism more acceptable because its underlying assumption is that women can be feminists without fundamentally challenging and changing themselves or the culture.'
bell hooks, *Feminism is for Everybody*

This chapter will discuss women's work and activism, activism among lesbian and bisexual (LB) young women and how feminism has been interwoven with all of the above. As hooks explains in the quote above, feminism is something that is, and very much should be, constantly changing, evolving and challenging. When there is too much of a shift from one side to the other, for example from being a very community-based movement all about sisterhood and solidarity to an every-woman-for-herself approach, or as hooks describes it, "lifestyle feminism", does this mean feminism starts becoming a little diluted? If so, how does this 'new' idea of feminism impact on work with girls and young women, a practice that is shaped by community and conversation, and does it have a place at all?

Feminism: is a collection of movements and ideologies aimed at defining, establishing and defending equal political, economic, cultural and social rights for women.

In principle young women's youth work is:

- helping and actively encouraging young women to have a voice
- based on the current interests of young women, while offering new challenges
- able to tackle global and closer-to-home issues around sexism, lesbophobia, biphobia, racism and ableism in the world in an accessible way
- able to challenge gender stereotypes by letting young women know they can pursue male-dominated careers and become mechanics, engineers, pilots, scientists if they want to
- inclusive of young women who don't 'fit in' with mainstream or expected 'girliness'
- always doing something a little bit radical and different and acknowledges that all young women are also a little bit radical and different in their own way

lesbophobia: is an irrational negative response to lesbian women based on the fact that they have sexual/ strong emotional relationships with other women.

biphobia: is an irrational negative response to bisexual women based on the fact they have sexual/ strong emotional relationships with both men and women.

People can also experience lesbophobia and biphobia if they are presumed to lesbian or bisexual but are not.

IS A WOMAN'S PLACE A SAFE SPACE?

It's important to acknowledge privilege and oppressions when working with young people. Lesbian and bisexual young women experience what some people have called the 'double-glazed glass ceiling', the sister to the 'glass ceiling' idea, which you may or may not have heard of before.

Glass ceiling: An invisible but real barrier through which the next stage or level of advancement can be seen, but cannot be reached by a section of qualified and deserving people. Such barriers exist due to prejudice on the basis of age, race, ability, political or religious affiliation, and/or gender. It applies to both social and employment advancement.

Oppression: When a person or group of people who have power use it in a way that is unfair, unjust or cruel against people on grounds of race, sexuality, class and disability. In a protest and activism setting you may have heard people talking about not wanting to feel 'held down' by higher powers, this is referring to oppression as a feeling of being weighed or pressed down by something.

Without using too many fancy words, 'double-glazed glass ceiling' means that someone is dealing with two lots of oppression and here the term is used to describe the fact that LB women are dealing with sexism in their daily lives and also les/biphobia on top of that. There are also young women out there who are lesbian, BME (Black and Minority Ethnic) and/or also disabled, and it is important

Left: Rock Against Sexism, from Paul Patrick's personal collection

Mansplaining: (slang) A combination of the words "man" and "explaining" that describes the act of a man explaining something to a woman with the assumption that she knows less than he does about the topic being discussed purely on the basis of her gender.

to acknowledge the great impact that these multiple oppressions will have on their lives. In response to this, young women's work has placed an importance on creating safe spaces for their young women to be themselves, discuss their sexuality and talk critically about sexism, without fear of judgement and 'mansplaining'.

A 'safe space' may mean somewhere to go that is less likely to put someone in danger, somewhere to be yourself and a place where there are ground rules that ensure group safety through respectful actions, language and attitudes. Safe spaces for women were essential to allow groups to grow and to create a place in which women's voices could be heard, especially in LGBT activist and community spaces that historically were not always inclusive of women. As a result, tensions and conflicts arose between the Gay Liberation Front, Women's Liberation and lesbian women who aligned themselves between both groups. Often women's needs came second. Paul Fairweather, a Manchester Councillor and LGBT activist, remembers the tensions:

'I mean originally the plan was to have a separate lesbian centre, … there was a pot of money put aside to build or to set up a separate lesbian centre, and the lesbian centre sub group met and looked, and looked for various buildings. And my

Right: Lesbian Strength, 1982, from Paul Patrick's personal collection

colleague [Chris Wood] who was a lesbian officer was very involved in that, but there wasn't, we weren't able to find a suitable site to build or to set up a lesbian centre. And when the Gay Centre was being proposed, because it was quite a significant amount of money, there was a lot of hostility in the press locally and nationally. So when this was built and set up it was, it became more of a lesbian and gay centre, and I think there was an attempt to try and make it actually, there never was a lesbian centre separately, so actually, I think more women began to use the centre. But the plan was to have two centres, a lesbian centre and a gay centre.'

Geoff Hardy, an original member of the Gay Liberation Front (GLF), talked about similar conflicts that occurred within the Greenwich Lesbian and Gay Rights Group between lesbians and gay men and how he feels he would have responded to the same challenges today:

'I think it's a power thing too, you know, certainly in my generation and I think it probably is changing, but men were schooled to be outward and women were not schooled in the same way. So men would just take the floor and talk and we men would do that and then the women started getting pissed off and saying, "Hey, you're not listening." And in those days we just didn't see it and we thought they were bolshie, bossy, were words that came to mind, you know, and nobody would, now I'd go, "Would you say that of a man?" No. But, so I think it was quite right that they pulled away also because they were dealing with feminist issues as well as lesbian issues. Were they women first or lesbians? You know, they were also taking lesbianism into the feminist movement, that was quite a struggle. So I think it was a very difficult, enormously wealthy time of learning.'

There is something unique, special and intimately invaluable about shared experience. Having the opportunity to disclose our lives with other people who have been there and lived through the good, the bad and the uncertain times too is important. Amelia Lee, a youth worker

Above: Gay Liberation Front Support, from Paul Patrick's personal collection

explains why that's true for her:

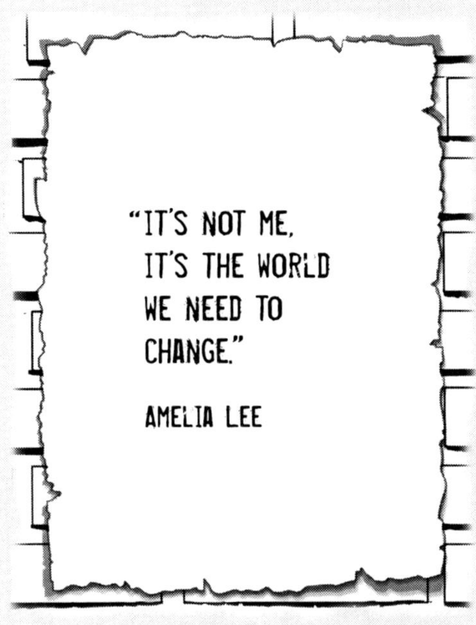

'When you talk to other women and you get that they feel the same too you think actually it's not me, it's the world, it's the world we need to change because me and all these women can agree on the fact that things aren't equal. And I think that's the great thing again that youth work can do and youth work should be doing in more places including schools really.'

Outside of the GLF and women's liberation groups, LB women and youth workers were busy trying to create women's spaces, communes, movements and support systems so that women like themselves could unite and motivate one another in times of difficulty and success.

Jan Bridget, a working class woman from Lancashire, worked in factories then joined the Royal Air Force for six years before completing a Diploma in Youth and Community Work. Her first youth work position was with Lancashire County Council as a rural youth worker, however she was forced to leave due to homophobia in her workplace. This was well before it was illegal to

Jan Bridget is an LGBT youth worker, now retired, with over 25 years experience. Over two decades she has conducted research, developed training packages, produced resource materials and run LGBT youth groups. She even has an award named after her – The Jan Bridget LGBT Youth Worker of the year, presented each year by LGBT Youth North West through a public vote.

discriminate on the grounds of sexual orientation. Jan and other youth workers made many attempts to set up lesbian-only youth groups in Leicester and East Lancashire but faced many barriers; lesbophobia from the council, ejection from the women's centre for being 'too lesbian' and also opposition from the gay centre who disagreed with there being a lesbian-only youth group. However, in the early 1990s, following further opposition from Lancashire County Council, yet another lesbian youth group was closed. Using research they had gathered from setting up the group, Lesbian Youth Support Information Service (LYSIS) was established. LYSIS was a long distance support network for isolated young lesbians around Britain which ran for six years and supported hundreds of young LB women.'

Here is an excerpt from the *Young Lesbians Coming Out Pack* published by the Lesbian Information Service in 1996 that explores some of the difficulties in coming out as young women and the sorts of things young women could expect to hear in their daily lives that may stop or deter them from coming out:

'When (if) we ever learn about Lesbianism (falling in love with other females) it is in a negative sense: We hear school-mates (and sometimes we join in) calling a girl "LEZZIE", maybe because she has chosen not to have a boyfriend or has short hair or has refused to be feminine (wear make-up and dresses). To be called "LEZZIE" is to be insulted. Lesbianism is rarely, if ever, mentioned in sex education.'

The interview below was conducted with workers and young women from the Islington Young Lesbian Group (IYLG) for the magazine *GEN*. The interview was also published in the IYLG Coming Out Guide. This passage describes what activities the young women got involved with and how they defined themselves. Interestingly, at the beginning of the interview, when the young women's group are asked who they are, IYLG members insisted that: 'WE ARE not trendy feminists who wear DMs and lots of badges.'

'One young woman had come to the meeting for her first time. She had read about Islington Young Lesbians in her *Spare Rib* diary a week before. The group has been meeting for approximately eight years. It survives on donations and very little funds. One of the group members told me that they had received an anonymous donation from an old woman. "I reckon she was a lesbian" she said. "What do you do?" I asked. "Scrambling, camping, football, charity walks," the group replied. Their list went on for nearly five minutes, the group had even been to Amsterdam for a week last year. At meetings they play pool, listen to music and sometimes have 'heavy discussions'. The staff supervise, offer support and help the young women with any problems.'

In 2003 the Young Women's Health Project was formed, since then it has gone by a few names, but has been widely known as Lik:t or Young Women's

The main aims of the Young Women's Health Project are to improve young LB women's health by promoting various activities designed around six areas of wellness which are: physical, emotional, intellectual, spiritual, occupational and social/community.

Group (YWG). The group, based in Manchester, provides a place for young LB women to meet, take part in activities and sessions run by and for young LB women.

As well as youth work sessions, the group regularly created, published and distributed their own magazines, posters and handy guides for other LB women. For some young women, the group was and is still a safe haven where they could be themselves, one young woman said "I like Young Women's because it's small and feels safe". Something really special about YWHP is that it is its own constituted group. This means that young women are members and there is also a committee with roles that are filled by young women, sometimes supported by a youth worker. Within a committee there are a few roles: there is a chair, who is someone that writes an agenda for meetings and keeps everyone on task, a secretary who might type up notes from meetings and emails them to members and a treasurer who looks after the finances. This is a good example of young women's work that encourages young women to take an active role in running the group whilst gaining skills that could be used in many areas of their lives.

Myrtle Finley, a youth worker who volunteered with YWHP in the early years of the project, reflects on her memories of the group what her roles were:

'In the young women's group which we called Lik:t then, I was involved in helping steer the project, so there was a group of young women that were involved in planning and developing the project and the workers supported it. So you know, we created magazines, we organised events, we did summer camp, and all those things. So I got involved in lots of different things over

Zine: Pronounced 'zeen.' An independently or self-published booklet often created by a single person or produced collaboratively as part of a group, collective or cause, about a particular interest or topic.

those few years after I started.'

Young Women's Camp, 2014

As previously mentioned, YWHP have produced their own magazine, also known as a zine, the *Lik:t Magazine.* The group created and distributed several issues a year, each with a particular theme, message or purpose. For example they have created magazines focusing on sex and relationships, International Women's Day, drugs and alcohol, radical women, mental health, music, sport and a review of winter camp and or summer camp.

A long-standing tradition for YWHP is a weekend residential Summer Camp. In the past there were biannual summer and winter adventures. Sarah Gilston, a young women's worker who was involved with the group, describes her memories of the annual Young Women's Summer Camp:

'My main favourite times have been on the women's residentials, just the whole people coming together from all over the country, some people we'd never met before, and just sharing stories. 'Cause you spend that much time with people, and it's such a lovely calming atmosphere, and you're sharing kind of things with each other and the different activities that you're doing, and so gradually people start to feel so comfortable with each other. And, you know, … it feels like a massive group at the beginning; they always say this don't they, the more you get to know people the group gets smaller. And I just remember it being such a lovely atmosphere, and really everyone looking out for each other, you know, everyone doing their bit with washing up and cleaning, and just telling stories round the fire and just the breadth of the different, you know, different activities that went on. They were just, oh it was just perfect, just had some good times.'

FEMINIST AND LGBT YOUTH WORKERS ACTIVISM

Being an activist can take on many forms, and for young LB women that can start anywhere. They might set up their own young women's group or take part in activities or behaviours that many people in heterosexual relationships take for granted (such as holding hands with a partner in the street or being able to casually mention their girlfriend in a conversation) without fear of being judged or even attacked. Even the act of coming out to yourself as a lesbian or bisexual woman, or a woman who loves women is powerful and important. Even talking with other women about what's going on in the world and questioning, evaluating and rethinking parts of life and behaviours in people that seem 'normal' or 'usual' can be considered activism, as Amelia Lee explains:

'I think it shows what you can use and work with in youth work, so campaigning and being activisty isn't necessarily holding a placard and marching down the street. Sometimes it's about day-in day-out in a youth club having these conversations, talking about the media, talking about what we see and what we don't see in the media, analysing what's going on. So not just seeing it for what it is but thinking where is, where is the hidden story?'

Some youth workers used traditional methods of protesting such as writing protest songs to help educate their young women about feminism, being safe on the streets and raising awareness about street harassment, like Ali Ronan:

'We wrote a lovely song called 'Women Should Be Safe to Walk the Streets' and that was, you know, that was in '88 or something so you think, yeah, that was fun. Stuff about LGBT activism I think things have changed a lot since the mid '80s because I think now there are specific groups, like the one the woman here is running in Wigan or in Manchester, where there are groups where young people feel that it's a safe place where they can come and talk and be themselves.'

For other women, being an activist means holding placards in marches, getting out there onto the streets, organising demonstrations and being involved in direct action. Sue Sanders, teacher and LGBT activist, shares her experience of being a young lesbian who was exposed to a wide world of possibilities when she began to get involved with politics and activism:

'That whole process of the lesbian feminist movement and the women's movement meant I became much more comfortable and things were much more exciting and political. I mean, sexuality became political. I mean, my first years with Faye were... very challenging, very difficult. It was not a good relationship, but it was the only one I could find at the time. But as politics

came into it, I then found most of my lovers in the political context, in political campaigns, in movements, and that was a much healthier place.'

Maeve Bishop, feminist activist, recalls:

'I've done quite a lot of stuff around like sexual assault and abuse and trying to combat that or change the views of the public. So I helped to organise - I don't know if you were around then but I helped organise the Manchester Slut Walk, which I understand there are like problematic connotations from it, but it was really cool. There was like 800 women or something who were all kind of standing up together to say we can do what we want and it's never our fault if we get assaulted, and stuff like that.'

Not just going out and campaigning for what could be defined as 'women's issues', feminist and LGBT activists were also present at anti-apartheid marches, peaceful protests, pit closures and the campaign for nuclear disarmament. As Lena Milosevic, teacher and LGBT activist, remembers:

'Was it just the NUT [National Union of Teachers] conference? Oh there was a lot more because actually for a lot of women who were radical, who were feminist, who were lesbian in the '80s, there was a lot to fight against. If you were opposed to nuclear proliferation, you know, there was a whole movement and environment to campaign for nuclear disarmament, CND [Campaign for Nuclear Disarmament], it was massive. Women, who were pitching their tents and living outside Greenham Common, you know, trying to prevent the American expansion of nuclear cruise missiles, for example, in the UK. There was a whole lot there to be active against. There were the miners, the pit closures, you know, closing our mines in the '80s. So again there was a whole load of activism to be done around that, around LGBT, around anti-apartheid

Greenham Common Women's Peace Camp was a peace camp established to protest nuclear weapons being sited at RAF Greenham Common in Berkshire, England. The camp began in September 1981 after a Welsh group, Women for Life on Earth, arrived at Greenham to protest against the decision of the British government to allow cruise missiles to be based there.

movement. And many women, including myself, were involved in all of those. So we campaigned against apartheid, we campaigned against the pit closures and against nuclear proliferation and arms and cruise missiles and so on.'

While feminists have rallied in solidarity with a number of different causes and movements, there are still areas that they disagree on. Two contentious issues in some spaces are discussions concerning the rights of sex workers and the inclusion of trans* women in women-only spaces. Amelia Lee, a youth worker, explains:

'I think in feminism there's a group of people that are very much about censorship and about no prostitution, making it illegal or certainly making it illegal to buy so not, you know, not persecuting the women but persecuting the punters, the men. And then there's another group of women that are more into what's called sex positive, so do believe that the real true path of freedom is about sexual liberation and we should all be very much more chilled out about everything to do with sex and I think they're not always talking at opposites. Sometimes there's some useful bits of both sides of it.'

Women–only spaces, and how welcome trans*women are to them, remain a contentious issue in some activist circles. Some activists seek to deny trans*women access to women-only spaces. They do not recognize the self-identification of trans*women as women. Others believe this exclusion to be transphobic and unnecessary.

Young women's work and particularly work with LB women will always be important as long as young women grow up in a world where they are exposed to sexism, lesbophobia and biphobia. It is important to keep spreading the word about feminism, increase the visibility of LB women and keep talking about young women's work and how important it is. Many young women will now come across feminism for the first time on a website, or through social media and most likely speak with other LB women online before ever (knowingly) meeting one face-to-face. Therefore, as well as the valuable face-to-face youth work, it is essential that youth groups and feminist organisations have a presence online, wherever that may be.

Feminism cannot and should not aim to serve one kind of woman alone, who holds more power and influence than the rest. Individualist feminism should not be the lasting image of feminism, or held up as the sustainable answer to engaging more women in the movement. Working together will make feminists more resilient and informed. From sisters and trailblazers of the past and the hard work of LB women, youth workers and feminists in the present who encourage women to participate in change, there is a chance that the world could be different and a much better place for women in the future.

Where in the world are there other women like me? Prepare a list containing a mix of famous and 'everyday' women.
Here are some well-known and lesser-known women you might like to use. Some of them openly identify as lesbian, bisexual and/ or trans*, others do not. Feel free to edit the list or use examples that are more relevant to you:

Jackie Kay
Dusty Springfield
Anne Lister
Kate Bornstein
Sarah Waters
Alice Walker
Angel Haze
Carol Ann Duffy
Sue Sanders
Angela Davis
Marsha P. Johnson
Frida Kahlo
Tegan and Sara
Kelly Holmes
Steph Houghton
Claire Harvey
Sally Ride
My grandma
My mum
My best friend

MY LIST:

ARE ANY OF THESE WOMEN RECOGNISABLE/KNOWN AS LB OR TRANS WOMEN, AND IS THAT IMPORTANT?

IN WHAT OTHER WAYS ARE THEY LIKE YOU AND IN WHAT WAYS ARE THEY DIFFERENT TO YOU? (THIS COULD BE SOMETHING THEY ARE 'KNOWN FOR' I.E. THEIR JOB, TALENT, BELIEFS, ACTIVISM, OR PERSONAL STYLE.)

WHAT WORLD DID THESE WOMEN GROW UP IN AND HOW DOES THAT COMPARE TO THE WORLD WE LIVE IN NOW?

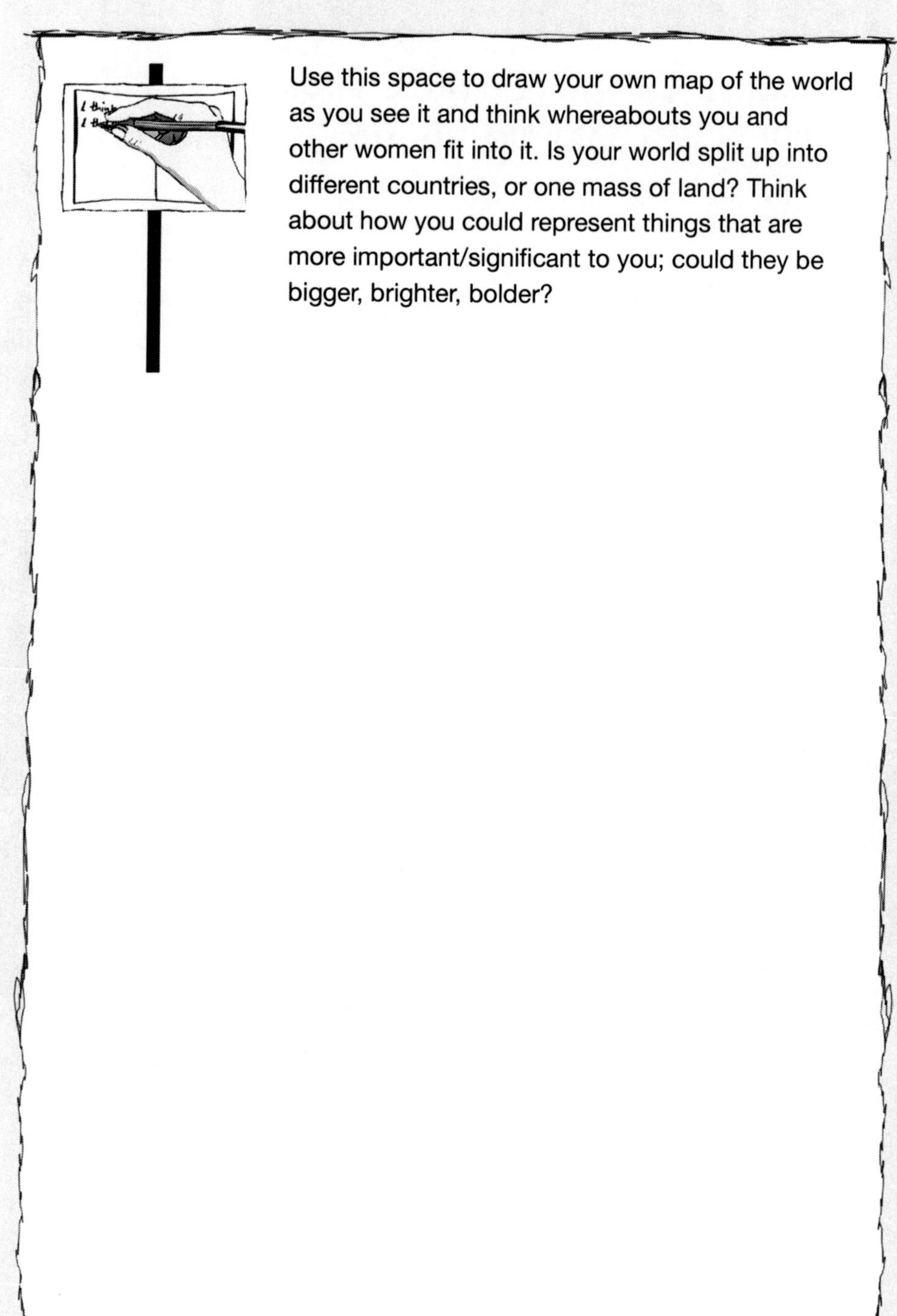

Use this space to draw your own map of the world as you see it and think whereabouts you and other women fit into it. Is your world split up into different countries, or one mass of land? Think about how you could represent things that are more important/significant to you; could they be bigger, brighter, bolder?

CHAPTER 10

OUTNESS: TO BE OR NOT TO BE

CLÍODHNA DEVLIN

'I'm gay'. The infamous words of Ellen Degeneres, from her TV show *Ellen,* reflect the words spoken by many people coming out as lesbian, gay, bisexual and/or trans*. Like Ellen, coming out to family, friends, and the community may feel just as exposing as in her T.V. show, when she was heard over a speaker by a whole airport full of people, and also on air by over 40 million people worldwide!

Fast forward to 2014, and when a celebrity comes out, it's hard not to hear about it. Recent examples include Olympic medallist Tom Daley, whose coming out video has already attracted 11 million views. Similarly, half a million followers read actress Raven Symone's tweet celebrating being part of the LGBT community. Actress Ellen Page chose to come out while speaking at the *Time to Thrive* conference. The video of which has been watched over five million times on YouTube (as of September 2014).

For a number of those interviewed in this book, their sexuality and/or gender identity was made extremely public. Lena Milosevic, Tom Robinson and Peter Tatchell came out in public forums whilst Section 28 was in operation. This was met by both hostility and celebration, which may be still similar to the experiences of those coming out in 2014 despite changes in legislation.

WHY DO LGBT PEOPLE COME OUT?
IS IT ABOUT FEELING READY?
IS IT BECAUSE THEY WANT TO SHARE AND CELEBRATE THEIR IDENTITY WITH OTHERS?
DO THEY CHOOSE TO, OR DO THEY FEEL THEY HAVE TO?

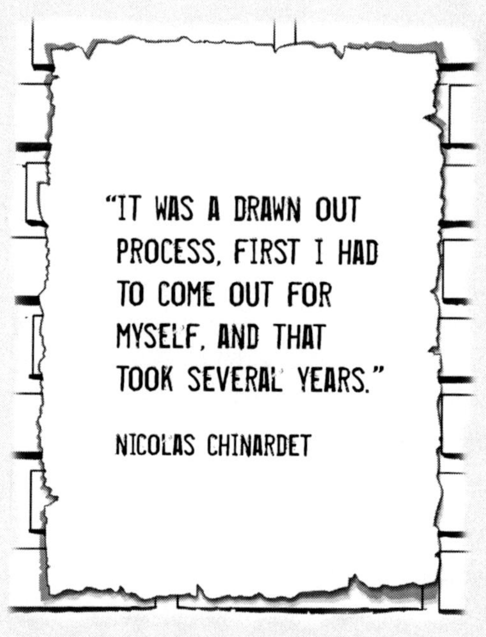

Describing the moment she came out to her class, teacher Lisa Blake described how it felt physically to say the words:

'I had built it up so much, it was like a lifetime of thoughts and words and also struggles and hopes were coming out, as well as my sexuality. I was sweating, I was shaking, I went all red.'

This chapter will consider the experiences and impact of coming out on the activists involved in this project. It is important to note that the experiences and stories are difficult to compare to others. While each was unique, it appeared that for every person interviewed, the process of coming out to others was just the tip of the iceberg. For many LGBT people, coming out takes time. Activist Nicolas Chinardet remembers:

'It was a drawn out process, first I had to come out for myself, and that took several years.'

According to the research 'How You Can Help Us' by LGBT Youth North West 2014, a high number of young people described having "always known about, they were attracted to people of the same gender, and/or questioned their gender identity from a young age". Youth worker Sally Carr agrees:

'Yeah, I guess from the age of four I knew I was different to the other girls at school and it was only when I got older that I got the language to describe that, and that language was lesbian.'

Many of those interviewed were able to pinpoint the moment or moments that helped them to understand their gender, sexuality and/or identity, however, many also described how the lack of conversation and education led them to hiding this, like John Vincent:

'I knew I was gay when I was tiny…I grew up in the '50s and '60s when there wasn't any talk about it. So I knew I was gay, but I didn't actually come out until my mid 20s.'

Jeff Evans also discussed the difficult process of coming to terms with his own sexuality, based on what he had heard about being LGBT:

''Cause I'd heard the term homosexual, and with that term homosexual came a lot of shit.'

The internal struggle, questions and fears (described in the iceberg image), met with external judgements and responses, lead many people to feel distress, shame and like they had something to hide.

Coming Out: The tip of the iceberg, by Cliodhna Devlin

Singer Tom Robinson discussed the enormous difficulty he felt as a young person identifying as gay and how this changed over time:

'Having nearly tried to kill myself at 16, you know, preferring to die rather telling anyone else I was gay. In my 20s after I'd kind of come to terms with myself and who I was, and the fact that I liked men, I went to the opposite extreme and literally made a song and dance about being gay.'

WHAT MAY HAVE CHANGED FOR TOM ROBINSON THAT MADE HIM FEEL MORE COMFORTABLE ABOUT HIS SEXUALITY?

WHAT MAY HELP PEOPLE TODAY?

Coming out to others may be a next step for many people. and telling a close friend, family member, a few or many people can be that step. For some, this may never happen, and it is important to note that it is okay to not come out to individuals, or anyone, especially if it does not feel safe to do this. Coming out is not always a desirable or possible goal for a multitude of reasons. For example, some Muslims who use the Joyce Layland LGBT Centre in Manchester have a goal of living an LGBT life, while at the same time not revealing this aspect of their lives within their Muslim communities. This example could be applied to people of many different faiths and life situations. Some people also choose abstinence (deciding not to have sex) as way of reconciling their conflicted identities.

Peter Bradley, a teacher and member of the Gay Liberation Front describes his understanding of the individuality of coming out:

'I've never thought coming out as something you force people to do. It's pointless. If you don't feel comfortable, what's the point? So even in Gay Liberation, which was very much in your face, a very, sort of saying to people, hmm, come out. Even in Gay Liberation people recognised that we're all different, that we all come out at different stages. Some people never do. Everyone has their own way in the world. So that was very powerful as a set of ideas for me.'

Many activists highlighted that for them, there was an internal dilemma about coming out. Coming out for many was considered a 'political statement' and some may choose to call coming out a form of activism.

Some people choose to tell everyone at once. Some people choose to tell specific people first, in order to guage reactions, 'test the waters', and again feel safe.

Not everyone will come out to their family and friends. Not everyone will have the opportunity to and be able to for various reasons. However, for a high number of activists in the book, their families have been integral in their coming out journeys.

Lena Milosevic recalls having to assess the impact on herself and others of coming out during school, eventually waiting until she was in Further Education to come out:

'I can remember there were one or two friends that I kind of came out to first. And that was all great, they were great… but it was just like very small numbers... baby steps before you can run. So there was support and I just think that is so important still today for everybody really. We need to feel we're alright and accepted and loved.'

Sally Carr agrees with Lena Milosevic, describing this need for love, alongside the spectrum of reactions many parents have when their child (or children) comes out. While much has changed for those coming out in 2014, Sally is extremely aware of the difficulties many young people face:

'Young people are coming out at younger ages and parents don't have a rule book …There're a lot of issues [for young people]. Coming out is one of the biggest ones we know of. Coming out is the hardest. And for them to come out to their parents, some have got really good parents, you know, understanding parents, and they'll say, "I already knew".'

Lena Milosevic understands how it can feel to not be accepted by a parent:

'I think that the most difficult has been my own family's attitudes to my lesbianism. My mother and my father particularly, but my mother particularly who hasn't accepted it, full stop. That's been the most difficult. Parents can take a sort of one step further and be supportive and for example go, "Yeah I'm proud of my son because he's gay." You know, I think that is just, that rocks.'

Similarly, Peter Tatchell was very aware of how his parents would react to his sexuality, and he understood that approaching this carefully was important for him and for them:

'Because of my parents' extremely devout faith I knew that simply blurting out to them, "Hi mum and dad, I'm gay," that would not work, it would be too much of a shock for them, and they wouldn't be able to handle it. They might even report me to the police.'

While there have been numerous changes and advances in laws to protect the LGBT Community, individual responses and actions are difficult to predict and then deal with. As a youth worker, Sally Carr still witnesses how parents' reactions to sexuality and gender can have massive consequences for young people:

'There's some that go, "Well, that's it then. You can leave, you can pack your bags, you can go tomorrow." You know, and there's such a distance between parents.'

For some activists, the experience of coming out to their parents was more positive. Maeve Bishop remembers:

'I just knew it wouldn't be an issue with them. I'm so lucky in that, so I didn't bother in coming out 'cause I just was like, "Well, I don't talk to you about my sex life or my romantic life," do you know what I mean? It just wasn't a thing that we talk about so I only told them when I was seeing someone who I was like, "Oh, you might meet this person because they're seriously in my life now."'

It is interesting to note how many of the activists interviewed felt a responsibility to take care of those they were coming out to more than they felt compelled to take care of themselves. John Vincent remembers:

'People have said subsequently that you know, in 1973/'74 it was a big brave step, and I suppose it might have been, but I felt it was the right thing to do. And I didn't want to go into a job where I was misleading anybody.'

Maeve Bishop's experiences were mostly positive. However, she did have an experience in which she felt she had to come out, or 'tell the truth'. She remembers hearing, "you've not told me that you're gay and you just don't trust me enough to come out."

This feeling of 'misleading someone' and having to come out may be caused by heterosexism.

Heterosexism is the idea that everyone in society is presumed to be heterosexual. In 2013, LGBT Youth North West launched the Don't Assume campaign, encouraging people to consider the assumptions they make about people, including their sexuality and gender identity. These assumptions can lead many, including the activists in this book, to feel a pressure to come out, but also to feel 'different', 'unusual' or 'wrong'.

This campaign stemmed from staff and young people in the organisation dealing with assumptions and judgements about their gender, sexuality and identity, however, it was discovered during the project that a similar phrase had been used in the 1970s by the Gay Activists Alliance. Their statement was "How dare you presume I'm heterosexual".

One activist, Peter Bradley, remembers wearing a badge with this statement, and considering other people's reactions:

'Well, you have the choice, you always have the choice to shut up and/or lie about it [sexuality]. So to me, ... coming out nurtures me. .... I've just suddenly remembered my poor late mother. One of my brothers was an actor, studied drama here at Manchester, and was in the Contact, doing some play in the Contact, and my mother and I came up. And I was wearing a badge, a pink triangle badge, saying, "How dare you presume I'm heterosexual" And as the train was coming into Manchester station my mum said, "Take off the badge, take off the badge," and of course I didn't.'

For many of the activists, and for many of the LGBT Community like Jayne Mugglestone, coming out did not

Don't Assume Campaign sticker, LGBT Youth North West

always have to be verbal:

'Holding hands with my partner was a way of me proudly saying I'm LGBT, without actually having to say it, you know?'

However, it is important to consider the assumptions made, for example, when a couple are holding hands. Would you automatically assume that two women holding hands both identified as lesbian? Would you assume that one or both of them may identify as bisexual or pansexual? Do you need to know how they identify? These questions may help people to question their assumptions, rather than the person's identity, and also support the LGBT community in feeling a pressure to come out and label themselves (if they do not feel comfortable \ in doing so).

Geoff Hardy remembers a time when the magazine he was reading "outed" him and his sexuality to colleagues:

'I would take in a copy of *Gay News* to read simply 'cause I hadn't read it and I thought I'll take it into school, part of me also thought this is a good thing to do. So I'd be sitting in the staff room reading it [laughs] and I remember one time somebody saying, "Why do you have to flaunt your sexuality the whole time?" So I looked up and I said, "Sheila, what's that on your fourth finger on your left hand?" "It's my wedding ring." "Why do you have to flaunt your heterosexuality?".

Badges, stickers, wristbands, symbols and physical gestures, or indeed verbal comments can be methods of coming out to others. Ultimately, activists wanted those who were considering coming out to feel safe in doing so, and some of them have dedicated their lives through activism, or their careers, to supporting others.

Above: How Dare You Presume I'm Heterosexual, Gay Activists Alliance, Australia, from Paul Patrick's personal collection

For many of the teachers interviewed, their own coming out experiences encouraged them to consider how they could ensure that students did and do not have the same experiences in school that they had.

In chapters 4 and 5, 'Section 28 Section: Twenty Hate' and 'Promoting EdYOUcation', many different elements of education were discussed. In relation to coming out and education, many activists specifically highlighted their experiences as young people, but also as professionals in education.

For Tony Fenwick, witnessing particular incidents in school made a decision for him about whether to come out in school:

'As a young teenager in that situation I knew that if I was gay I had to keep my head under the parapet, the safest thing was to keep it in the closet.'

For many young people, their experiences in school will shape their understanding of the world, and for LGBT and non-LGBT young people, school is a place of education. This education should include and raise awareness of LGBT themes and issues, as well as empower individuals and challenge behaviours and language. Peter Bradley remembers his time in school:

'When I was at school, secondary school, in the '60s, there was absolutely no mention of, I mean, even homosexuality was just, in my whole six years I never heard the word once, and it was a bit early for the word lesbian and gay. But just the term homosexuality was never mentioned on the curriculum.

A lack of education, added to the lack of challenging of homophobic, biphobic and transphobic language, meant that young people felt unsafe, unimportant, and uncertain of where to go for support. As recently as 2002, Brian Jacobs felt this not only as a student, but as a teacher, with a lack of consistency from colleagues in challenging language and behaviour:

'You know, I'd be walking down the corridor and I'd have the word "gay" shouted at me umpteen times and, wherever possible, whenever physically possible, I would stop a child in their tracks.

'[Some would say] "He's so gay," and if that happened in a classroom or in the corridor I challenged it if it was physically possible and so with the help, I mean I wasn't there on my own, lots of other teachers were also challenging it, but I was probably the, probably one of two or three that challenged it every time whereas the majority of teachers probably didn't challenge it every time.'

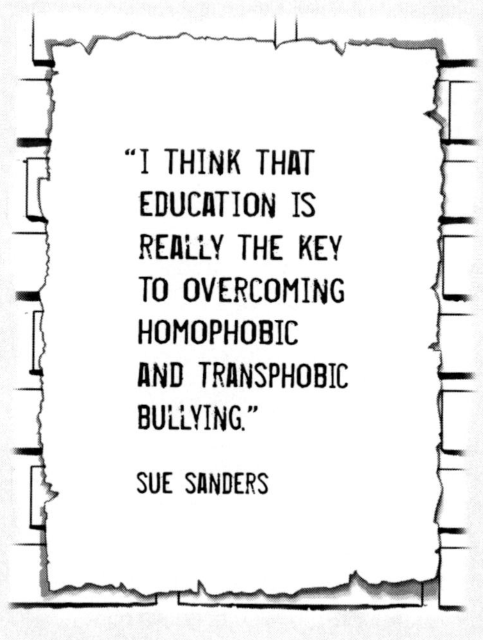

In 2014, despite massive changes in legislation, policies and the end of Section 28, Sally Carr still recognises gaps in many educational settings:

'I think as educators, I think we need to be in that loop to sort of like cushion that blow but also to listen to what those young people say, because it's important to listen and to try and give them some encouragement. I'm unsure about what schools are actually doing in their curriculum for LGBT young people, but there's too many that I know of who have had bullying issues at school that haven't been dealt with.'

Having worked in education for many years, and founding LGBT History Month and Schools OUT UK with a number of the activists interviewed for this project, Sue Sanders believes strongly in the need for education of staff and students in schools, in order for the school to be a safe environment for all to be themselves, whether they are out or not.

'Now I'm not saying pupils who, you know, abuse other LGBT pupils should be prosecuted, but certainly action needs to be taken, certainly that needs to be challenged, they need some sort of disciplinary steps taken. But most importantly they need education about the issues, they need to be informed, they need to be engaged, they need to be challenged, they need to be forced to understand the adverse impact of what they are doing and saying. You know, and I think that education is really the key to overcoming homophobic and transphobic bullying. Not so much the threat of disciplinary action, although there's a place for that and it is necessary, but really to change hearts and minds, that's the key way forward. To provide a safe, welcoming environment for LGBT staff and pupils.'

Education and challenging language and behaviour is vital in terms of creating a safe environment for many. However, throughout the interviews, the term 'role model' was used repeatedly. The activists considered the importance of role models for themselves, but also how they may be role models to other people.

"I THOUGHT I WAS THE ONLY ONE, NOBODY WAS TALKING ABOUT IT... IT WASN'T, YOU KNOW, THERE WERE NO ROLE MODELS."

KELLY PARISH

Trans* actress Laverne Cox recently challenged the idea that she was a 'role model', introducing the phrase 'possibility models':

'I hate the term role models but I love the term possibility models, because women like Sylvia Rivera, Marsha P Johnson and Candice Cane made it possible for me to think it was possible to live my dreams.'

Typing in 'coming out' into any internet search engine will produce hundreds of videos, blogs, web pages and support links. Whether it is someone online, an LGBT person in everyday life, or a celebrity, having someone to look up to is thought to be as important now as it was to many of those interviewed, like Brian Jacobs:

'I think if you're going to be a teacher and you are LGB or T, you should be considering that you should come out. … I think the choice should not be whether should I come out but should I stay in the closet. I think that's the way people should be thinking, because you are a role model.'

It is important to ensure your own safety if considering this, and again highlights the importance of support from an organisation and workplace to do so.

Peter Bradley shared an experience of how he became a possibility model for a student, having had a difficult time coming out at the school he taught in:

'A few years later, a pupil in that school said, "Could I have a quiet word with you?" I said, "Oh yeah," because they often do that with, you know, an essay or something like that. And I said, "Oh sure." And he said, "I want to tell you I'm gay and how important having you as a teacher has been." And I just thought, well, that's one of the positive things that you find in a situation like that, that... Yeah, how you affect, things you do for your own benefit affect other people and we don't know where they end. And, you know, an effect you might have, something you do or say to people today, 20 years later they could come down and say, "That's the most important thing that happened in my life."'

For Liam Mason, a teacher didn't have to publically come out to support LGBT students:

'I was very lucky actually, one of the tech support staff, 'cause I was very into the technical side of drama and things like that, was also a lesbian, so even though she wouldn't provide me with advice or anything but she provided me with like sort of silent support. So I was very lucky in that respect that I had someone there who was there for me if I needed it, and a lot of young people don't have that. So yeah, I think that gave me that confidence to just sort of speak out.'

Tom Robinson, like Brian Jacobs, hoped that his coming out would help others:

'For my generation, Bowie, even though he may have been just pretending, it didn't matter because we got the benefit anyway. We got the benefit. For the first time in our lives queer rock and roll fans could listen to this music and go "that's about my life." It's not almost about my life, or about I know something of what that feels like, except the pronouns are wrong. It was actually about my life. Fantastic feeling that was. And I did swear to myself that if I ever got in the position that my own music got a wider audience that I would try and do that for other people.'

Until lesbians and LGBT themes and issues became more visible, and representative, to Sue Sanders, it was difficult to come out internally and externally:

'There ... [was] nothing on television. I was seeing nothing, you know. My concept of a lesbian was, I made the mistake of reading Radcliffe Hall *The Well of Loneliness*, and that is not a good book to read when you have no picture of what a lesbian is. It wasn't really until feminism came along that, and that whole process of the lesbian feminist movement and the women's movement, that I became much more comfortable and my sexuality was much more exciting and political.'

"I THOUGHT "I'M THE ONLY GAY PERSON IN THE WORLD" AND THERE WAS NOBODY ELSE AROUND, AND I DIDN'T THINK THAT WAS A POSSIBILITY OF A LIFE FOR ME."

KELLY PARISH

Steve Bonham considers the impacts of lack of representation of LGBT people in the media, in public and in personal lives:

'Well if I look back at the mid 1970s when I came out as a gay person there were very few positive images of gay people, ever around you. While there are more role models now for young people, I'm sure it is still very difficult for them.'

This invisibility may impact on whether someone is able to come out, and how safe they feel when doing so. For many, there is a feeling of being different, not normal and alone, as Janet Batsleer has witnessed:

'There are still young people growing up who face a sense of being the only person who has those experiences, feelings, desires.'

Coming out is not an issue that solely concerns young people though; youth workers volunteers and practitioners were also fighting their own battles and feelings of confusion about their sexuality. Jayne Mugglestone, who has been involved in youth work for several decades spoke about how being involved in youth work with strong women role models helped her to come out:

'I was around loads of really strong women doing the young women's work. So in Coventry there was loads, there must have been about 20 odd girls' groups all around the city and it's not a massive city, and we would have massive events with like a couple of hundred girls coming to these kind of city wide events. So there was all these youth workers, there must have been about 30 or 40 women youth workers running the groups. Most of them actually were

straight, but they were so, erm, they were just really, really good role models as women. And then there were few lesbians as well and I think that was brilliant for me. So I followed them around quite a bit, sort of making friends with them and thinking, "Oh I'd really like to be a lesbian." [Laughs] And then in the end thought, well no, I can be, it's not, I think I'd just been brought up, like we all are to a degree, aren't we, culturally, to think oh well, you know, you're just straight, especially in those days, so it was quite a big jump for me to think oh, yeah well, okay. But yeah, it made it really, really easy to come out 'cause everyone was dead supportive and I'd just seen all those positive women, I suppose, and positive lesbians.'

While education, legislation, and possibility models can help the process for some individuals, often coming out isn't a one-time thing. Some people will be doing it for the rest of their lives. Someone new may assume you're straight and you'll have to decide whether you come out to them and if you do, how. This can be quite overwhelming, and is something many activists discovered after having first come out. Lisa Blake realised this, and having come out to family, friends, and more recently her school, she spoke about how this felt:

'The whole coming out situation is a strange one, isn't it, because it's not a once and forever thing? You come out once and you think, "Oh, thank goodness, that's over, I've done it." you know, but then somehow it all subsides and you have to do it again, and sometimes you do and sometimes you don't.'

Clare Blake agreed:

'Coming out never stops does it? It's again, and again, and again.'

The variety of experiences in coming out (or not coming out) highlight the difficulty in discussing a process that is not straightforward and comparable for everyone. But, by being out at work, people like myself have managed to create an environment in which young people find it easier to be out and proud of themselves. Such a lot has changed in the past 50 years. During the lives of many of the activists interviewed for this book, LGBT lives have gone from illegality to protection in law.

Many of the activists, therefore, were keen to share advice to young people today about coming out. While for some, their gender, sexuality and identity may always have to be kept to themselves, or only shared in certain safe arenas. Tom Robinson wanted to reassure young people today, that for some, it does get better:

'I just would have given anything aged 15 for somebody to have said to me, "It gets better." That's the wonderful thing about the It Gets Better campaign is that adults are putting themselves on the line, on video, famous ones, not famous ones just going online and going, "This was what my life was like, it got better."'

Peter Tatchell shares a piece of advice about coming out to his own parents, but states that this could apply to anyone:

'So my strategy was to, what I call the drip, drip, drip affect. So I would drop hints, so if there was some item in the newspaper about a gay person that was derogatory I'd say, "That's really wrong, discrimination is not a Christian value." My parents would sit up and, or if there was a report, there was a gay rights march in London or New York or wherever I'd say, "I think that's really good, whatever you think about homosexuality they shouldn't be persecuted." You know, "One of my co-workers at my job was gay and he's a really nice person, what's the problem?" So gradually over a series of months and a couple of years my parents put one and one together and came up with two, or in this case came up with gay! So what happened is they made the approach. When they felt comfortable and confident they asked me outright, "Are you gay?" To which I of course said, "Yes." But you know, at the time and ever since my parents always said that was a really good way to come out. They say they would never have been able to emotionally and psychologically cope with it if I'd just come out at the age of 17.'

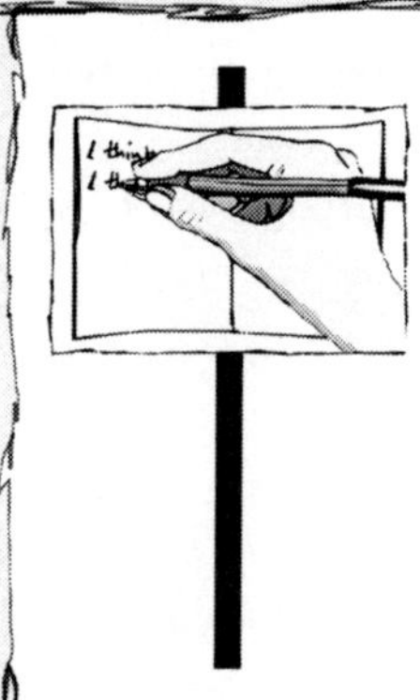

Below is a space to write a coming out letter. It could be to yourself, or to others. Have you ever had to come out about anything? This could be about your gender, sexuality, mental health, addictions, about something important to you. You can share this with others, or keep it to yourself, but know that behind this letter is support and encouragement from the activists in this book.

CHAPTER 11

A FRIEND OF A FRIEND OF DOROTHY

AMELIA LEE

'If you fight on your own issue only, you get nowhere, not really… because we live in one world, and we belong in this whole world.'
Geoff Hardy, teacher co-author of *Schools OUT UK* book.

This chapter is about the allies and friends of the LGBT movement – how LGBT activists have also been involved in many other campaigns and issues and how friends and allies have impacted on LGBT activism history. We sometimes also call these people SOFFAS.

A Friend of Dorothy: (Slang) A coded way of saying someone is gay, and was used as code when male homosexuality was illegal. It is thought to have come from the character Dorothy in the *Wizard of Oz* film, who is considered accepting of all the different people she befriends in the film, including a camp lion, and has become a gay icon.

Ally/ Allies: People, groups or states that have joined or associated with each other for mutual benefit, to achieve a common purpose, or in support of another's cause.

SOFFA: an abbreviation that stands for Significant Other, Friend, Family or Ally and usually applies to someone connected to and supportive of the LGBT community.

LGBT activists, like lots of other types of activists, often get a passion for justice (making things more fair) that leads them down a number of paths. Their activism rarely concerns just LGBT issues, but lots of other types of campaigning too, as Jayne Mugglestone remembers:

'Every weekend we were on marches: protesting about Clause 28, and

the Alton Bill (about changing women's access to abortion). These marches were often on at the same time... And the miners' strike was happening at the same time. The British Army was in Ireland where there was almost civil war, so we went on Troops Out Demonstrations. At the same time Nelson Mandela was locked up in South Africa, then the Poll Tax... there was loads of stuff going on.'

LGBT people and LGBT activists come from all walks of life (across all classes, all races, all religions, all abilities and geographies), so when activists met about one cause, they sometimes got inspired by another cause. Just as LGBT people found themselves getting involved in other people's causes, in doing so, they also got lots of other people involved in the LGBT cause. The recent film, *Pride*, has brought to much wider audiences the ways in which lesbians and gay people supported the miners, their families and communities during the miners' strike. Geoff Hardy was an activist campaigning for these causes:

'In 1983/'84 there was a big miners' strike across the country and a group of us got involved with Lesbians and Gays Support the Miners and we adopted a valley in south Wales and we raised about ten grand I think, which was a lot of money then. At the next London Pride march there was a pink triangle donated by Lesbians and Gays Support the Miners [LGSM]. And a miners' wife, as they were known in those days, got onto the stage in Trafalgar Square and she spoke of her sadness and shame at the treatment that they must have given because of their homophobia. She was almost in tears and was talking about how they had unknowingly discriminated against their sons and daughters and people around them and then she said, "And then you did this for us, and I want to say that you lesbians and gay men are always welcome in our valley."'

Sue Sanders, who was involved in campaigns around the Stephen Lawrence inquiry describes her experiences:

Lesbian and Gays Supoort the Miners, London Pride 1985, from Everyone Out! Conference publication, 2011

'The Stephen Lawrence inquiry came up with a definition of institutional racism, and those of us had been working in the equalities field were, were you know, not surprised. Yes, at long last, it's about time people were talking about it, and were talking about the concept, not of, you know, people individually being racist but the fact that our very structures of how we organise ourselves in our institutions inevitably oppress people who are not heterosexual, white, able bodied, male and Church of England. I then built on the concept of institutional racism to talk about institutional oppression and say, look, most of our institutions were built by white heterosexual, able-bodied, upper-class men. They were building their institutions to be comfortable for them, forgetting they're not the centre of the world, except they are, of course. I delivered a lot of the training after the Stephen Lawrence Report, as every member of the criminal justice system, police officers, crown prosecution, judiciary, probation, all had to have diversity training, equality and diversity training, and built an alliance with Doreen Lawrence, Stephen's mother.'

The history of allegiances, as you will see from this chapter, is, by its very nature, messy. People who were activists across a number of causes have talked about how stressful it was, and how some of them experienced 'burn out' and stopped campaigning because their own physical and/or mental health was suffering. Many people were put off from getting involved in campaigning because of the arguments, in-fighting, time commitments, the impact of all the knockbacks and defeats or because they just wanted to keep their heads down and not get into trouble. For Peter Bradley, however, no matter how hard it got, the way he saw it was that there was no choice:

'One of the whole things about gay liberation is that the private should be public, the personal is political. So, who you sleep with, it's political because, if who you sleep with ends up with you being attacked or killed, then it's part of politics and it's an area where you change things if you want to survive.'

WHY WERE LGBT ALLIES SO IMPORTANT?

The Sexual Offences Act in 1967 made it legal for two men to have sex with each other (in private and as long as they were over 21 years old). Gay men aged under 21, therefore, were committing an illegal act if they had sex.

Throughout recent history there has been a strong association between shame and being gay and this was true in the 1960s and 1970s, even after the 1967 act, and is still true for many people now. LGBT people who grew up in the 1970s, for example, would have had parents who were around before 1967 when male homosexuality was illegal. They therefore might feel that to have a gay child would carry with it a sense of stigma or shame.

Thus, the consequences of being cast out by families and friends, the need for secrecy in sexual activity, relationships and everyday life in the face of criminalisation, and the fear of being outed at school or work, have meant that many gay people have relied on allies who have made a huge difference in their lives.

My Teacher – My Ally – by John Vincent

There was one teacher who I really, really rated, and he recognised I was having a difficult time, so he suggested I might like to volunteer in the school library. I'd already got a sort of Saturday job working in the public library, and so being in the school library kind of gave me something to do, something to get out of the hurly burly of the school at lunchtime … it was a really good thing for him to have done without saying why he'd done it, but he obviously recognised that I was being bullied and there were things going on. And I suddenly found that, you know, I was working with some

Keep your dirty laws off my body, from Paul Patrick's personal collection

people for example, who were much more supportive than I thought they were going to be. So I started to explore, I think quite late on and I think very fast, kind of who I was, and brought it out into the open.

It was hard for young gay men to find each other (let alone lesbians, bisexual or trans* people), so it was common to feel very isolated, or to have to leave your own town in search of the big cities (like Manchester and London) where you had more hope of finding other people like you. Some were lucky to find a 'Homophile Society', later called 'Gay Society', at their Student Union if they went to university. This was where finally they would find people like them.

Some gay men had parents who were supportive of their children's sexuality, and recognized that their children, as well as other parents, needed their help to break down isolation. One such person was Joyce Layland, as Peter Cookson, who attended the group in Manchester Joyce volunteered at, recalls:

'Oh Joyce Layland! One of the greatest human beings I ever met, she was fantastic. She formed the [Manchester] parent's group with Cath Hall, and my mum [Bernadette Cookson], and she just had nothing but compassion, she didn't have a malicious bone in her body. She never judged anybody, she had no prejudice against anybody for any reason. Everybody to Joyce was her best friend until they proved otherwise. So every day she was there it was great, I had many long conversations with Joyce.'

At a protest march against Section 28, Joyce spoke on the podium in front of 20,500 people and said 'I am the proud mother of a gay son.' The crowd roared with support. She was angry that such a normal comment would provoke such a response but she saw how powerful it could be. When she and the parents' group members spoke on radio or on television during that time, people took notice. Here were heterosexual parents saying "protect our

Abolish the Age of Consent, Revolution Youth, from Paul Patrick's personal collection

gay children from homophobia." She went on to create Family Pride in 1990, the national umbrella organisation for groups for parents of LGBT children. From 1991 this became known as FFLAG (Family and Friends of Lesbians and Gays).

Of course, one of the big reasons for having a parents' group, was to help parents who were struggling to come to terms with their child being LGB or T, and in doing so, to help the person who has come out to maintain a relationship with their family. Barbara Spence, who was a member of the Manchester Parents' Group, recalls:

'The joke tale is that everybody's sat around the table having Christmas dinner and you're just getting to your Christmas pudding and your 18 year old offspring announces, "Oh by the way mum I'm gay." And when they come back home at Easter (on a break from University) mum's still sat there with a Christmas pudding on a spoon saying, "Did I hear right?" So yes, parents do need help, some need more help than others. As human beings, as heterosexual human beings who are married and have children, the minute you hold a new baby in your arms you plan their whole life ahead for them. You see this wonderful white wedding and then the children and the big house, two cars, all the rest of it, and then now when they get to be a teenager that image is shattered. And some people can cope with it, and others can't, so we try to be there for the ones who can't quite cope with it and we say, "It does seem a long dark tunnel at the moment, but where do you want to be with your children? Do you want to be behind them, do you want them to just disappear off the face of the earth, or do you want to stand by them and say, "This is my son, or daughter, this is what I produced, this is what they are and I'm proud of them?"'

In Manchester people like Paul Fairweather and Joyce Layland also helped form a gay youth group, which eventually had its own staff member, Nigel Leach. As Nigel put it:

'Your parents need their own space, the young people need their own space, it's about inclusivity, making our services more open.'

STRONG PASSIONS, STRONG CONVITIONS, BIG DIFFERENCES: THE G THEN THE L THEN THE B THEN THE T...

Parents' groups, like most people in society, were getting used to the idea of gay men existing, and working out how they felt about it, but didn't have lesbians, bisexuality or trans* identities on their radar. Likewise, it took a while for some gay men, like singer and radio presenter Tom Robinson, to join the dots and begin to realise that they needed to support lesbians too:

'You can't ask for freedom for one minority, but not allow it for others. So you know, you've got be a feminist if you're a gay male activist. You've got to be anti-racist if you're a gay male activist, you've got to be pro-unions, you know.'

Similarly, Nigel Leach recalls:

'At the gay centre, I remember vividly lots of conversations about moving it away from the gay, from a male-dominated gay centre, to involve more women for example. So, you know, there wasn't an elite group of gay men at the top running things.'

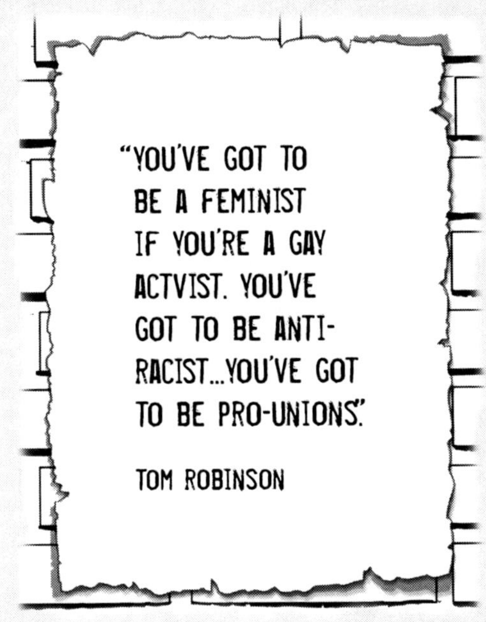

The impact of feminist movements on a number of women in the 1970s and 1980s gave rise to more women coming out and lesbian identity becoming more visible to the outside world. There were heated and sometimes very destructive debates amongst heterosexual feminists about how lesbians should be involved in the movement. Would having them on board dilute the feminist cause or make it seem too edgy/ dangerous?

There were fractures within the movement and in the 1980s

and 1990s, and there were some groups of lesbian separatist feminists, who believed that the only true feminists were those who rejected men and focused their lives as well as their political efforts on women. Of course, for every out lesbian, you can be sure that there were nine or ten women who "would be" lesbians, but were still living in the closet and feeling forced into conforming to what society was saying women should be: wives and mothers.

The allegiances between lesbians and gay men were prominent from the 1960s onwards, and were cemented by campaigns and fights that brought them together in solidarity. For example, many lesbians supported and cared for gay men in the 1980s and 1990s who were affected by HIV and AIDS, and fought alongside their gay male comrades against Section 28.

Many groups were renamed from 'gay', to 'lesbian and gay.' At the same time, with the support of the trade union movement, bisexual visibility emerged. In 1984 there was the first BiCon, a conference for bisexual people. From the 1990s, Student Union LG groups started to become LGB groups, and many other LG organisations followed suit. Bisexual people in these groups, however, reported (and still do today) feeling biphobia and bisexual invisibility within these groups.

Manchester's first gay centre was home to the TransVestite/TransSexual Group (TV/TS)) in the 1970s. In spite of this commitment to activism and support, the needs and priorities of trans* people remained on the margins of LG campaigning and visibility. At the start of the 2000s, the focus shifted to including trans* people more explicitly within many support groups and campaign organisations of LGB people. However, some LGB people felt that to include gender alongside sexuality issues would "muddy the waters" of their own campaign priorities.

March down Whitehall, Christine Burns

The work of Christine Burns, Stephen Whittle and other key people from Press for Change resulted in the introduction of the 2004 Gender Recognition Act, providing rights for trans* people to change their legal gender. Christine talks of how she led a Pride March in London and saw people looking at her thinking 'Who is this woman and why is she leading our march?' They were unaware of what a key role she had just played in civil rights for LGBT people.

By 2010 it was common for more groups to refer to themselves as LGBT, and then the job began of ensuring that trans* people's identities and needs were understood and genuinely catered for in these settings. The current emerging work is building allegiances with those trans* people who don't fit within the gender binary of "male" or "female". Non-binary, third-gendered or non-gendered people do not enjoy many rights under the law, unless they artificially put themselves in the "male" box or "female" box. For example, in legal terms, marriage is not defined as legal partnership between two people, but rather between a man and woman, man and man or woman and woman, so what happens if you are not a man or a woman, and/or in a relationship with someone who is not a man or a woman?

THE TRADE UNIONS STORY: FROM JERSEY WITH LOVE...

When we look back on the past 50 years of LGBT activism history, it is easy to see the Labour and socialist movements as friends of LGBT people, especially because of the legal gains LGBT people have seen under a number of Labour governments. The relationship between left wing/socialist movements and the LGBT community has not always been a happy one however, as some of these stories will show. Firstly, youth worker Liam Mason:

'I was the NUS Wales LGBT Officer, and I learned a lot from the NUS. They deliver quite a bit of training and LGBT awareness and are about action and change. They could learn a lot from youth work though, because they need to listen and engage more with the grassroots to actually implement a lot of the change.'

The more radical left wing movements of 1970s and 1980s, including the Socialist Worker Party and the Youth Section of the Labour Party, considered being gay a "bourgeois deviance" and were dismissive of it as an identity.

For active trade unionist Jeff Evans, who was from a family of miners and was a joiner by trade, the idea that how he was feeling inside was connected with

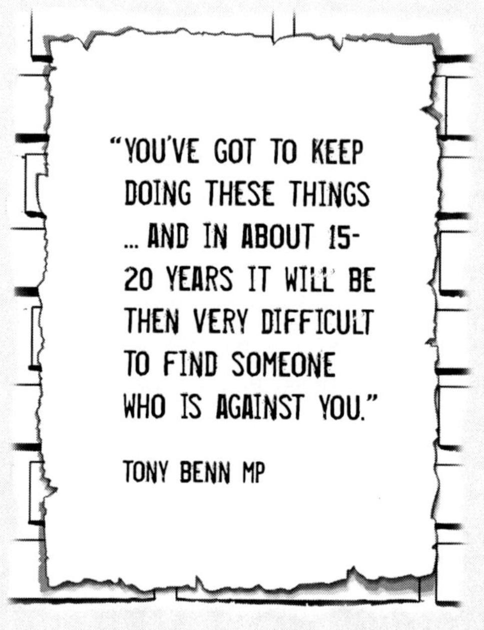

some sort of upper-middle class "dalliance" was both confusing and aggravating:

'And I remember speaking at a number of fringe meetings, and I was an apprentice joiner, so it was very hard to describe me as bourgeois in those terms, you know, I was a worker, speaking on a platform in favour of lesbian and gay rights. In the early 1980s at the Labour Party lesbian and gay fringe event, John Shires said Tony Benn MP sent his apologies but then a figure came through the crowd and it was Tony Benn! He stood up and apologised for sending his apologies, but there'd been so much nonsense in the press he felt he had to come along. And he made a very short speech that made an impression that I can almost remember it verbatim. Essentially what he said was you've got to keep doing these things. And if you keep going, in about 10 years there'll be silence, there'll be a lot of silence, but you keep pushing. And in about 15 to 20 years it will be then very difficult to find someone who is against you. And you're very sceptical, but here's a man with incredible experience, a former senior government minister, a member of the cabinet giving this advice out, and I was a teenager at the time. And that always stuck in my mind.'

Gay teachers founded local gay teachers groups, which then became the national Gay Teacher's Group. In 1983 this group became Schools OUT UK. The reason they formed together was because their own unions were not very supportive of them.

Handmade badge in support for gay teachers, from Paul Patrick's personal collection

There was a tipping point when the largest teaching union, the NUT (National Union of Teachers), decided to host their annual conference in Jersey in 1983. Jersey's own law stated that homosexuality was illegal, so the delegates that were gay men and lesbians were understandably surprised and outraged that the NUT would host their conference there.

Alan Jackson, an activist and teacher, recalled what happened at the conference:

'The outgoing president welcomes everybody and there is a vote of thanks to the welcome given by the official dignitary e.g. the mayor from wherever you're having the conference, and this is usually just a purely formal vote of thanks. But what happened on this occasion was Peter Bradley put in a card to speak against this motion of thanks, which was of course unheard of, and he began by saying that, you know, as a teacher, a trade unionist and a gay man…and of course the President of the Union who was chairing the session ruled it out of order and Peter eventually had to leave the podium. And that was the start, and of course then it made the press. It made quite a stir. … By this time we had quite good links left in the union and rank and file Socialist Teachers' Alliance, so we had their support.

Then at the first disco on the Saturday evening, which was the young teacher's disco, we asked that people dance with a member of their own sex, and people did. And at another disco later on at the end of the conference that happened spontaneously. We didn't plan that but it happened.'

Peter Bradley recalled how the unions changed and improved in response to some high profile cases of teachers coming out as gay and being sacked for it:

'John Warburton came out and lost his job, and that was 1974, and it resulted in an eight year campaign. Eight years is an awfully long time to be plugging away, but the solidarity of our Union after our initial battle with them helped. And now I am very proud of my union (the NUT), which was just so homophobic when I started, and have had a dramatic shift in position where they now have a LG space on the Executive reserved for a lesbian or gay man, so we are represented.'

Here are some activists recalling some unlikely allies that they have encountered during their lives:

UNLIKELY ALLIES?

The Priest's help – Tim Lucas

'There was a local priest who actually turned over his house as an HIV/AIDS support centre and they used to do lunch every day so people could get something cooked for them and have at least one good meal a day.'

Training the Police in South Africa – Steve Bonham

'[The police in South Africa, post- apartheid] were very receptive to LGBT training and it was quite interesting because they were genuine in wanting to change. The leading police officers organising it were all probably in their fifties and had been there policing for the brutal years of apartheid, crushing demonstrations. But these were people who decided not only was it in their best career interest to stay with things and the changes happening in South Africa, but that they were quite enthusiastic and wanting the rethink and re-evaluate.'

The Local Authority – My Ally? Terry Waller

When the gay centre support was agreed by the Manchester Council (to the tune of about £178,000) there were battles raging in the Manchester Evening News about whether Council money should be spent on it. This was during the early stages of Section 28 being discussed, so the Council had to take legal advice on whether it could support the gay centre. Some people did get frightened, others in the Council did try to sabotage it, and they succeeded in reducing the amount of funding for the build, but people like Val Stevens and John Nicholson remained solid supporters of the project and by 1989 the gay centre on Sidney Street was built.

Homosexuals seek support of union

The Daily Telegraph 5 April 88

By Our Education Staff

AN ATTEMPT to commit the National Union of Teachers to support "constructive" presentation of homosexuality as "an integral part" of teaching in all schools was launched at the union's annual conference yesterday.

In the first conference debate on homosexual rights in the union's 118-year history, homosexual delegates claimed that about 10 per cent of school pupils were homosexual and needed to see adult homosexuals and lesbians as "role models".

Miss Lena Milosevic, a Leicester teacher who said she was a lesbian, won a standing ovation from many delegates after saying she was taking a "considerable risk" with her career by speaking out at the conference.

Attacking the Government's proposal to ban local authorities from promoting homosexuality in schools, she said it was "offensive" that homosexual teachers should have to lie about themselves to pupils and colleagues or face the possibility of disciplinary action.

She also condemned "heterosexism", which she defined as "staffroom whispering when I talk about the good weekend I had with my lover".

Supporting the proposal for use of "truthful and constructive" material about homosexuality in schools, Miss Susan Burrows, from London, said it was "essential" that such teaching reached primary school pupils as well as those of secondary age.

For the NUT executive, Mrs Pat Hawkes said many teachers would require guidance on how to treat subjects such as history and English literature once the anti-homosexual provision in Clause 28 of the Government's Local Government Bill became law.

She also backed a call for members to be subject to the union's own disciplinary procedures if they were guilty of discrimination against lesbians, homosexuals or bisexuals.

The debate ended before any vote could be taken, though it may be resumed tomorrow.

Earlier, the executive opposed inclusion of a commitment to campaign against Clause 28 in its main education policy statement on the grounds that it would be "a distraction".

Some Left-wing delegates claimed that the clause would result in schools being uncertain as to whether they could use the works of Auden, D H Lawrence, Tennessee Williams or Shakespeare for fear that they might be construed as promotion of homosexuality.

Salaries on merit

By Our Labour Correspondent

Halifax Building Society is to link the pay of its 3,000 management staff to performance. The new system will replace general rises, due in August, and annual service-related increases.

Article from the Daily Telegraph, April 5th 1988, NUT Conference, Lena Milosevic Comes Out. Courtesy of Lena Milosevic

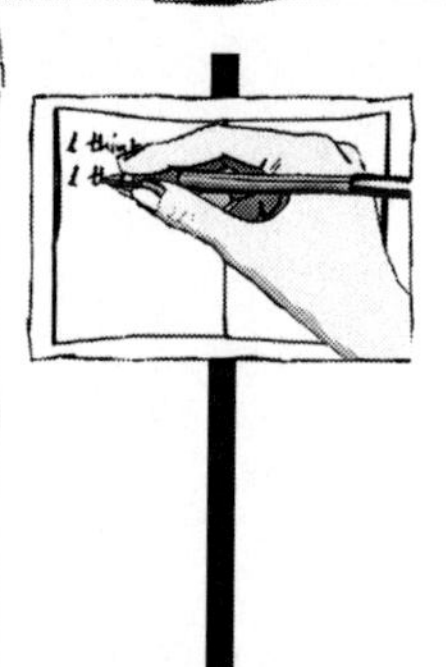

Who should be our allies now?
Think about the causes that LGBT people still need to take action on and write them here. Then next to them write down who you think the key allies are in helping with those causes:

Cause (something wrong in the world that we need to put right!)	Allies (who can help us bring about change)

Can you pledge one thing you will do to help build alliances between LGBT people and others?

My pledge is...

This relationships diagram or ally-agram includes a lot, but not all, of the activism that LGBT activists were involved in from the 1960s onward. ***Created in 'Ideas Sketch' by Amelia Lee***

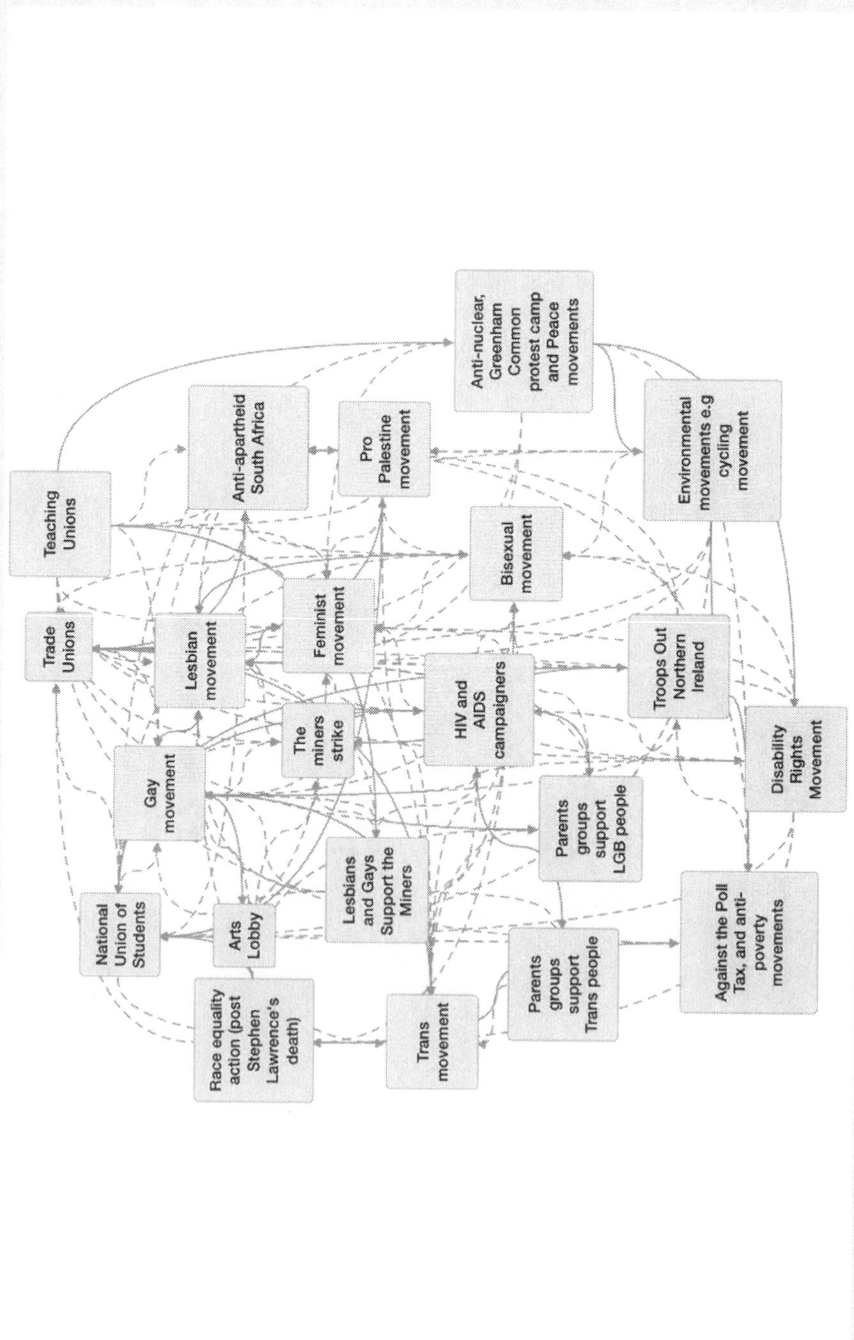

This space here is for you to draw your own activism map, we have suggested some links to get you started. ***Created in 'Ideas Sketch' by Amelia Lee***

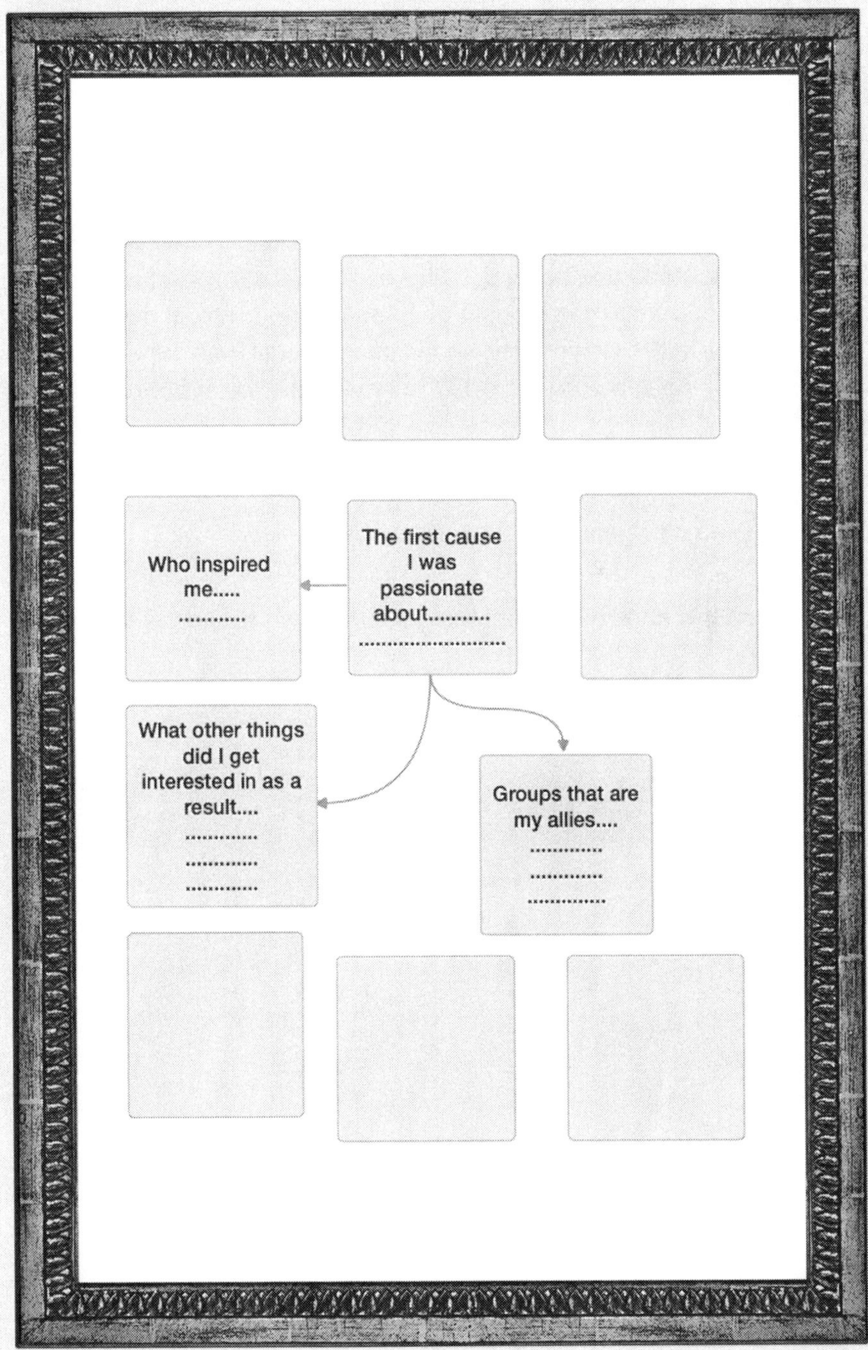

CHAPTER 12

IN EVERY ENDING THERE IS ALSO A BEGINNING:

WHERE DO WE GO FROM HERE?

YOU

This book has considered 'How We Got Here' and tells the story of LGBT activism in Manchester and beyond, however, there is still a long way to go. Activism from 1960-2000 has brought us to particular points, in politics, in education, in the LGBT Community, and in our personal lives. Where do we go from here? In the space on page 197, why not take the opportunity to write either:

- A hope or wish for where this journey will continue.
- A pledge you will make to help continue this journey,
  or
- A question this book has posed that you may wish to find the answer to.

A-Z ACTIVISTS

Alan Jackson

Alan Jackson was a maths teacher for 33 years, and during that time was active in the Gay Teachers' Group. Alan spoke at the 1983 NUT Conference "as a teacher, a trade unionist and a gay man."

Alison Ronan lectured in Community and Youth Work at Manchester Metropolitan University for 12 years, and is a feminist youth worker, recently completing a WW1 project with young women.

Alison Ronan

Amelia Lee

Amelia Lee works for LGBT Youth North West and the Empowerment People. Amelia is a feminist, socialist, co-operator and believes a better world is possible.

Andrew Dobbin was a teacher for 15 years and during that time experienced homophobia which was not dealt with by the school or board. Andrew joined Schools OUT UK in order to address this.

Andrew Dobbin

Barbara Spence

Barbara Spence is a member of Manchester Parents' Group, joining after her son came out nearly 20 years ago. Barbara has marched on Manchester Oxford Road with banners against Section 28.

Brian Jacobs was a teacher for eight years in a state comprehensive in Manchester, having been a lawyer for 40 years. As a teacher, Brian was an out gay man, not prepared to hide his sexuality.

Brian Jacobs

Clare Blake

Clare (right) teaches a class of five to seven-year-olds. After getting married, Clare came out to the class and parents, with positive reactions, and promotes tolerance through her work.

Geoff Hardy is a political activist, campaigning for LGBT rights since 1972. Geoff is involved in the Shropshire Rainbow Film Festival and remains optimistic that things can and do change.

Geoff Hardy

Gordon Smith

Gordon Smith is a youth worker with LGBT Youth North West. Gordon feels very lucky to have a job that enables him to help young people develop their own interests and personalities.

Janet Batsleer is head of the Community and Youth Work course at Manchester Metropolitan University. Janet has published a number of books, and enjoys working with young women.

Janet Batsleer

Jayne Mugglestone

Jayne Mugglestone has been a youth worker for 32 years and now focuses on sex and relationship education with young people. Jayne is passionate about everyone being able to thrive in life.

Jeff Evans is a passionate activist, an Academic Spokesperson for LGBT History Month, and is currently organising the 1st National Festival of Lesbian, Gay, Bisexual & Trans* History.

Jeff Evans

Jenny-Anne Bishop OBE

Jenny-Anne Bishop is the coordinator of TransForum Manchester which is a trans-mutual support and discussion and activist group trying to improve services in all areas for the lives of all trans* people.

John Cotterill, a counsellor, was involved in the Lesbian and Gay Switchboard in 1975 while studying at University in Preston. Through this, John became involved in the LGBT youth group at the centre.

John Cotterill

John Vincent

John Vincent coordinates a network of heritage organisations that work towards social justice. John is an out gay man who has just become a member of Schools OUT UK.

Lena Milosevic is the Country Director of the British Council in Mexico. In 1988, Lena came out publicly moving a motion at the NUT Conference against Section 28 and for LGBT rights in education.

Lena Milosevic

Liam Mason

Liam Mason is a Masters student, and recently got the job as the country's first publicly funded transgender specific youth worker, now working for the Young People's Advisory Service in Liverpool.

Lisa (left) is a teacher living in Nottingham, originally from Yorkshire. Lisa promotes respect for differences and addresses issues such as homophobic bullying with children in school.

Lisa Blake

Maeve Bishop

Maeve Bishop is a feminist, who during her time at the University of Manchester, did a lot of work and campaigning for the Sexpression Society. Maeve now works at LGBT Sidney Street Café and the allotment.

Myrtle Finley, a friendly vegetarian cyclist, grew up in Manchester with LGBT and feminist youth work providing the foundations of her study, and work as a bisexual community and youth worker.

Myrtle Finley

Narvel Annable

Narvel Annable is an author of several autobiographical novels, sharing personal experiences of homophobia, and experiences of peers who are no longer able to share their story.

Nicolas Chinardet is a French man who has lived in London for 14 years. Nicholas is a website manager and has been involved with LGBT History Month since it began, leading in social media.

Nicolas Chinardet

Nigel Leech

Nigel Leech studied Community and Youth Work at Manchester Polytechnic. Nigel came out in his late twenties, and became the very first sessional youth worker for the LGBT youth group in Manchester in 1985.

Nigel Tart is a teacher who has been involved in Schools OUT UK and LGBT History Month for over 20 years. Nigel has been involved in activist movements since studying at university in Leeds.

Nigel Tart

Paul Fairweather

Paul Fairweather moved to Manchester in 1978. He worked for the council as the Gay Men's Officer, and was heavily involved in setting up the Sydney Street building. He went on to become a local councillor for many years.

Paul Murphy is a former member of the LGBT youth group Lesbian and Gay Youth Manchester (LGYM). Paul felt that this was a space where he could be 100% himself, safe and comfortable.

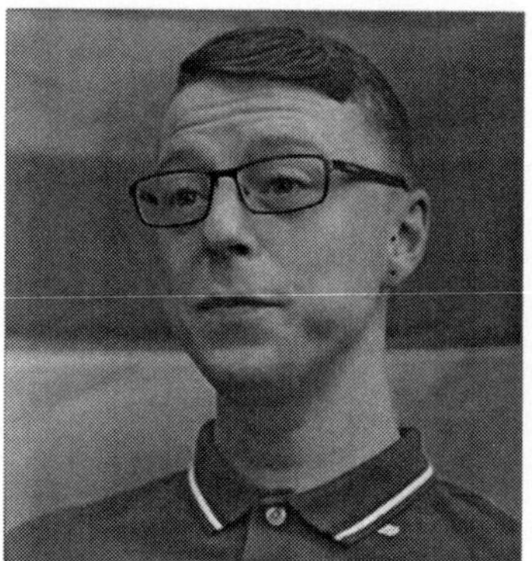

Paul Murphy

Peter Bradley

Peter Bradley was a teacher for 20 years, and was a member of the Gay Teachers' Group. As an activist he campaigned against Section 28 and has been involved in Schools OUT UK.

Peter Cookson is a councillor for Manchester City Council. After coming out in 1984, Peter attended the LGBT youth group on Bloom Street, where he met his long-term partner.

Peter Cookson

Peter Tatchell

Peter Tatchell has been campaigning for human rights for over 47 years. Peter is known for his campaigns for LGBT freedom, and is passionate about inclusive education in schools.

A lifetime LGBT rights campaigner and trade unionist, Pura Ariza currently teaches on the Secondary PGCE, Masters and Primary BA courses at Manchester Metropolitan University.

Pura Ariza

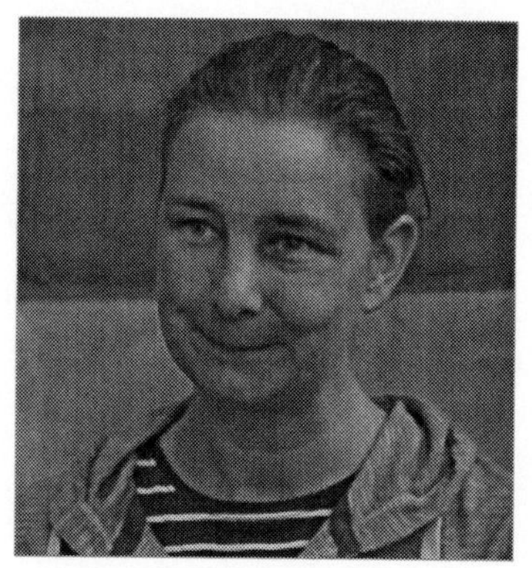

Sally Carr MBE

Sally Carr is a youth and community worker, working with a feminist perspective. Sally works to address and end inequality. Sally is the Operational Director for LGBT Youth North West.

Sarah Gilston joined Lesbian and Gay Youth Manchester in 2003, becoming the coordinator for the detached youth work project, Out and About. Sarah considers the LGBT Centre and the people in it family.

Sarah Gilston

Sam Cairns

Sam Cairns is a youth worker for LGBT Youth North West. Sam has a big interest in activism with a focus on international LGBT rights and law, representing LGBT Youth North West across Europe.

Steve Bonham was out as a gay man during his teaching career. As a chairperson for Schools OUT UK, and the early stages of the Gay Rights movement in Britain, Steve took part in Pride marches.

Steve Bonham

Steve Boyce

Steve Boyce is the Patron's agent of LGBT History Month, Schools OUT UK and The Classroom. Steve is an ex Head teacher, and passionate about campaigning for LGBT rights.

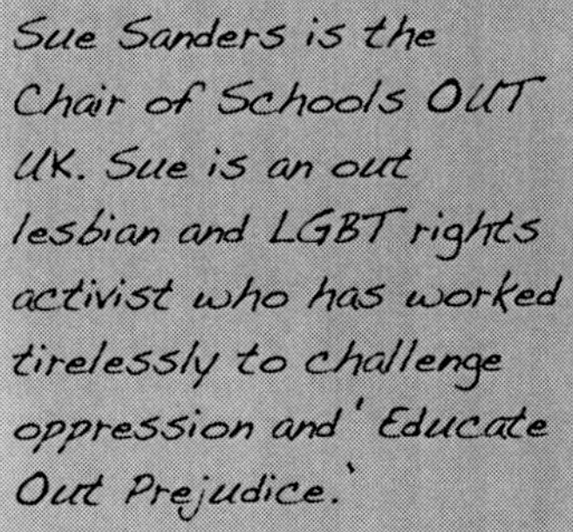

Sue Sanders is the Chair of Schools OUT UK. Sue is an out lesbian and LGBT rights activist who has worked tirelessly to challenge oppression and 'Educate Out Prejudice.'

Sue Sanders

Sylvia Kölling

Sylvia Kölling campaigned to keep the centre open in 2007. Sylvia and her partner founded the Queer Café in 2008, after frustration with the lack of provisions for specifically queer people.

Terry Waller has been a gay activist since 1972, was involved in the Manchester Gay Alliance, and founded the Switchboard. Terry was involved in the building of the centre in Sidney Street.

Terry Waller

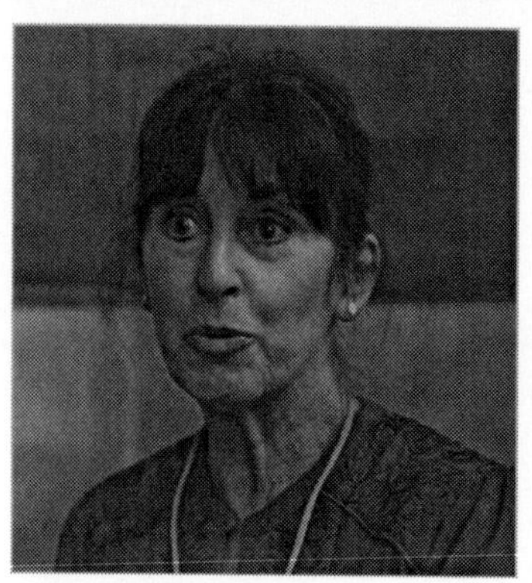

Therese Downham

Therese Downham works for Wigan Council, and currently works for the Be You Project in Wigan, a youth group for lesbian, gay, bisexual and trans* young people.

Tim Lucas has been involved in a number of LGBT organisations including Bristol and Brighton Switchboards and LGBT History Month and Schools OUT UK since 1975.

Tim Lucas

Tom Robinson

Tom Robinson is an LGBT rights activist and musician. In his twenties, after coming to terms with himself and the fact that he liked men, he 'literally made a song and dance about being gay.'

Tony Fenwick is a teacher in Hertfordshire who lives in Luton. Tony is the Co-Chair of LGBT History Month and Schools OUT UK, and has also been an equalities officer for the NUT.

Tony Fenwick

CONTRIBUTORS

We would like to thank everyone who has contributed to the book and project, through ideas, pictures, stories, articles and events. For your time, energy and activism for the LGBT Community, thank you.

To all the activists (please see 'Activists' section) who gave their time and shared their stories, and for those helping us to get where we are today.

To the young people and who interviewed the activists:

Alex Mason

Alice Dawson

Cael Hays

Charlotte Bolton

Dylan Hughes

Frank Holcroft

Jak West

Jake Watts

Josh Sheldon

Keeley Thomas

Luke Armitage

Molly Loughlan

William Frederick

Alice Andrews and the lovely team from Glasgow Women's Library who welcomed the Young Women's Health Project, educating and empowering us, and those who visit

Ali Hanbury for continuing to support the LGBT Community of Manchester, managing the Joyce Layland LGBT Centre, and for resources provided to the project

Amelia Lee for your activism, chapter writing, editing, advice, support, youth work and the most fantastic stationery collection

Claire Holmes and the wonderful staff and volunteers from Sidney Street Café who have provided incredible food for events and fuelled the team with vegan chocolate brownies

Clíodhna Devlin for project coordinating, chapter coding and writing and for being our invaluable leader on this project

David Alderson for education and contribution at the Schools OUT UK Conference

Debi Withers for proof reading and publishing the book at HammerOn Press

Eluned Cook for proof reading the book and design work for the play

Emily Crompton for your passion for what the Joyce Layland LGBT Centre was, is and will be

Erica Adkins and Naomi Austin from enJOY Arts who empowered our young people with their incredibly fun and informative sessions www.enjoy-arts.org.uk

Hannah Berry for chapter coding, writing and capturing the Centre beautifully

Heather Davidson for your interviewing skills and enthusiasm, always

Hebe Phillips for chapter writing, art and images, the mural and always pun-tastic chapter titles

Jess Marshall for photography and passion for the LGBT Zine Library in the Jaye Bloomfield Resource Library

Kate Sapin for your support, activism and for your passion in sharing your knowledge to educate community and youth workers and activists in Manchester and beyond

Kelly Parish for your interviewing skills and your dedication to LGBTYNW and the Joyce Layland LGBT Centre

Lucy Harding for your kindness, patience and respect when creating the interview films - www.vergemedia.co.uk

Kerry Cable for transcribing hundreds of pages of interviews incredibly quickly

Liam Mason for planning and delivery of the oral history training, for chapter writing and support to the project from the start

Lily Grey for chapter editing and continued support of LGBT Youth North West

Milly Shaw for your promotion of the events and project

Myrtle Finley for your interviewing skills, support of Wednesdays in the training

Niamh Devlin for book editing, proof reading, surviving “codeageddon” and for your passion for education and learning

Niamh Moore for your ecofeminism, planning and delivery of the oral history training, resources, education, chapter writing and for teaching us all a thing or two about youth work and world foods

Nicolas Chinardet for photography of events

Oliver Bliss for your interviewing skills, Tweeting and support of Wednesdays

Paul Patrick (see ‘In Memory Of’ section) for donation of activist badges from personal collection to LGBT Youth North West

Rachel Williams for your promotion of the events and project, and trialling lesson plans in schools

Sally Carr for your activism and passion which continues to inspire and empower

Sam Cairns for your interviewing and baking skills

Sue Sanders for your lifetime of activism

Tamzin Forster for being able to translate the million and one ideas the team had on to paper, and into the cover, design and layout of the book www.tamzinforster.co.uk

The Devlin Family -Patrick, Niamh, Odhrán and Aoife, for proof reading, consultation, support (and everything, always)

Tony Fenwick for chapter writing and creating lesson plans for the schools work

To the LGBT Youth North West trustees for all your support

To all the LGBT workers, teachers and allies who have helped us get here

To the groups who welcomed the team, helped with training in oral histories and taught us about activism in 2014:

Lesbian and Gay Youth Manchester

Wednesdays, Stockport

WYnotLGBTQ, Wythenshawe

Young Women's Health Project, Manchester

Heritage Lottery Fund

Joyce Layland LGBT Centre, Manchester

Manchester Central Library

Manchester Metropolitan University

Manchester Sound Archive

Glasgow Women's Library

People's History Museum, Manchester

University of Manchester for the support in the project, partnership in the Schools OUT UK Conference and resources

VADA Theatre

WITH THANKS TO...

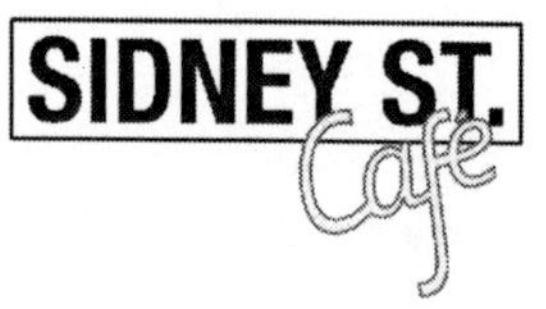

NOTES

This space is for your notes, ideas and thoughts...

Lightning Source UK Ltd.
Milton Keynes UK
UKOW04f0627220215

246606UK00003B/63/P

PREJUDICE AND PRIDE

LGBT ACTIVIST STORIES FROM MANCHESTER AND BEYOND